THE REALITY

OF

EVERYTHING

LINDSEY K. HAM SR.

THE REALITY

OF

EVERYTHING

The Truth...Speaks For Itself

LINDSEY K. HAM SR.

CITIOFBOOKS, INC.
3736 Eubank NE Suite A1
Albuquerque, NM 87111-3579
www.citiofbooks.com
Hotline: 1 (877) 389-2759
Fax: 1 (505) 930-7244

Ordering Information:

Quantity sales. Special discounts are available on quantity purchases by corporations, associations, and others. For details, contact the publisher at the address above.

Printed in the United States of America.

ISBN-13:   Paperback   979-8-89391-879-3
               eBook   979-8-89391-880-9

Library of Congress Control Number: 2025917711

TABLE OF CONTENTS

This book is dedicated to God in The Name of Jesus Christ. This book is dedicated to all of humanity. I am eternally grateful to God in The Name of Jesus Christ by The Holy Spirit for HIS wisdom, guidance, love, and absolute patience with me as I finally put this informative book together. Thank you Lord God....... The Creator of Everything!

This book is true. This book is interesting. This book is truly interesting.

PREFACE

God created everything including human beings for *His purposes*. Human beings ask "Why?" and "How?" about everything because we are each born *knowing* that there are *purposes* **for everything** in existence both good and evil, spiritual and physical. Since we already know that there are purposes for everything, we ask "Why?", and "How?" about everything to discover what those purposes are. The word "spontaneous" means that something has no purpose and that there is literally no reason for its existence, so if everything (including all life) is "spontaneous", then there would be no reason for us to ask "Why?" about anything .... yet we ask "Why?" about everything. Why?

All manifested matter in physical existence (both organic and inorganic) is literally made up of *purposefully functioning* atomic forces which are making up that matter; not to mention the matter itself having many purposes. Some people refuse to humble themselves to Almighty God even while existing in the presence of different interconnected natural functions always happening around us all. Winds, rains, nights, days, birds, seasons, grass, clouds, sunshine, etc., were all purposefully functioning before we ever existed. Spontaneity cannot produce purpose. Spontaneity cannot produce intricate, interconnected, very intelligently designed indeed, purposefully operating, interconnected systems and functions. We scientifically know that there is no such thing as "spontaneity". People claiming atheism say this existence is spontaneous, yet they KNOW that absolutely CANNOT be true. Science from every genre CLEARLY SHOWS that

God created everything, and there are dire consequences for blaspheming against Almighty God.

God knows what He is doing and when all is said and done, **every** knee **SHALL** bow, and **every** tongue **SHALL** confess that Almighty God (The Creator of This Universe) is The King of Kings and Lord of Lords (Romans 14:11; Isaiah 45:23 KJV; Philippians 2:8-10 KJV)! God is The Same God Yesterday, Today, and Forevermore.

We are individual human spirits (personalities) who are continually in contact with The Holy Spirit as well as demonic spirits as we operate *through* our physical bodies. This book discusses this reality as well as the differences between "religion", "science", and **The Truth** (which we all want to know).

CREATION CHRONOLOGY

GENESIS: CHAPTER (1)

Verse 1: God created Space and the Earth.

Verse 3: God created the Sun.

Verses 4 and 5: God spun the earth around to start the revolutions required to make nights and days.

Verses 6 and 7: God created the sky (the atmosphere).

Verse 9: God formed and separated the oceans, seas, and the dry lands.

Verse 10: God named the Earth.

Verse 11: God created the plants, flowers, trees, etc.

Verses 14, 15, and 16: God created the moon and the stars.

Verses 20 thru 25: God *spiritually* created each animal (there was no evolution).

Verses 26 thru 31: God *spiritually* created mankind; male AND female.

GENESIS: CHAPTER (2)

Verse 7: NOW God made man's *physical body* from the ground and breathed the already created male AND female *spirit of man* into that one body.

Verses 18 thru 20: Only NOW did God **physically make** the **already spiritually created** animals (this is why dogs act like dogs, turtles act like turtles, etc.). Adam (the man AND woman) then named each animal.

Verses 21 thru 25: God put Adam (male and female) to sleep and then **physically separated the woman from the man.** The **spirits** of both sexes were created **BEFORE** God made those **different** physical bodies to contain the spiritual men and women. Be *very careful* about calling God a liar by sympathizing with people claiming that God has made mistakes! That is evil blasphemy.

(CHAPTER ONE)
HUMAN CONSCIOUSNESS:
ATTENTIONAL AWARENESS

God is The Reality of Everything and The Truth does indeed, speak for itself.

There is a spiritual realm and there is a physical realm. Human beings are spirits created in the image and likeness of *Almighty* God and we spiritually reside in physical bodies in this finite realm. We are *all* the spirit of man, but we are *each* individual spirits existing in individual bodies. **Anything** we can see, smell, touch, taste, hear, or otherwise *physically* sense is not spiritual; it is physical, and everything physical has already been sentenced to eternal damnation because of sin.

What is this physical realm? If the sun was a basketball sitting in the end zone of a football field, then the Earth would be about half the size of a BB and would be circling that basketball from about the 30-yard line. Pluto would be about a mile away and would be about the size of a tiny grain of sugar. There are other planets (I choose to call them planets) in orbit around our sun as well which are far more distant than Pluto. Some of those "planets" have moons of their own, so whether modern scientists classify them as planets or not, that's what they are to me. They are doing the same things the other planets are doing; rotating around with their own moons as they orbit the sun.

Our entire solar system (all the planets going around the sun) is a microscopic "nothing" compared to the size of the galaxy (the Milky Way) it is in, let alone the rest of the universe. If we could go out into deep space and look back at our solar system, only the sun would be visible and it would appear as one tiny point of light out of hundreds of millions of other tiny points of lights located in what we think is a spiral shape of stars we have named the "Milky Way Galaxy". Our Milky Way Galaxy is only one galaxy out of an estimated 100 – 200 billion (+) galaxies out in the known universe, AND those galaxies are hundreds of thousands, multi-millions, multi-billions, and multi-trillions of light years apart from each other. How far is that? Some people are driving automobiles which have at least 186,000 miles on the odometer. This indicates the total miles the car has been driven since it was made and to attain that kind of mileage on a car, that car would have to have been driven regularly for at least four to five years at the very least. Light travels that far *each second* …. each second, light travels 186,000 miles, so if something is *one million light years* away from something else, it would take a beam of light travelling at 186,000 miles each second, one million years to reach the other place. Think about that, then think about the almost unimaginable expanse of this universe. God is.

As amazingly large as this entire universe is, that one little "tiny half-BB" called Earth going around our "tiny" star (the sun) is the only place where there is life. The Earth is the **ONLY** place in the entire universe where there is life … of any kind. Most human beings have no idea how special we are, nor "Whose" we are.

Not only is there life on, in, and over this Earth, but the Earth itself is alive. God gave human beings physical dominion over everything including all life on this planet, and we are the **only reason** anything else exists. It literally takes a physical realm the almost impossible size of this universe to contain us, and the proof of this is that we (as tiny as we are) understand so much about it. God ALWAYS knows what He is doing. Think about how much we each understand. That should help you appreciate the fact that it takes a place as large and complicated as this universe to contain multi-billions of us at any given time.

Human beings are NOT spontaneous, evolutionary, meaningless stardust which happened for no reason. That is *absolutely ridiculous.* We can observe and comprehend ongoing situations in front of us while listening to other conversations between different people going on behind us at the same time. At the same time we know "in the back of our minds" that we need to stop at that little yellow store on the way home and buy some eggs to make for breakfast tomorrow morning. We know exactly where we are and how to get to where we intend to go next, all while recognizing a high school classmate standing in the line ahead of us right behind that guy who looks like he's about to do something crazy. We know when our next car payment is due and who we want to vote for in the next election. We know exactly what someone said to us last night and how to cook a steak. We're watching our child as they move around while knowing what we still need to do to be ready for work tomorrow. We also know the kitchen sink is broken and the paint on the rails at work is the wrong color. ALL that kind of information and **much, much more** is always in each one of us, and we take for granted the realities of our incredible existence. We do not recognize who we are because humanity has gone astray.

Right now you recognize almost everything in your immediate vicinity right down to the smallest item. Not only that, but you know at least a little information about each thing. If you do not recognize something in your immediate vicinity, then it will quickly stand out to you as being something you do not recognize. You will wonder what it is and pay more attention to that item. We understand all kinds of information about all kinds of things as microscopic as we are because we are each spiritually created in the image and likeness of *Almighty* God. We are tiny "physical nothings", yet we spiritually know more than most of us will ever realize we do.

We have the capacity to calculate where things are in deep space and exactly where they should be located at any point in the future. We can also calculate where they should have been at any time in the past based on their current movements. We have figured out other information as well about all kinds of other matter, including all kinds of information about the multitude of different life forms here on Earth. Physically we are "microscopic nothings", but spiritually we are created in the image of "Micro-Macro Everything". Think again about how much each of us already know and how much more we each have the potential/capacity to know.

Think about how many people you know right now and how many more people you can remember. You know their names, what they look like, sound like, and their personality traits. Think about all of your personal secrets, the arts you know about, the different songs, mountains, your and other people's habits and talents, all the different colors and how to make them, the names of rivers and where they come from and where they go, the words you are reading and the fact that you CAN read. Think about the different sports, statistics, smells, and all the different means of travel you know about (driving, walking, jogging, biking, air, sea, etc.). Think about the academics (math, science, history, languages, etc.) you know. You know **all kinds** of things about past and present situations, circumstances, fashions, the planets, cooking, the years, makes, and models of cars, your jobs, your past and present co-workers, emotions, prices, tools, space, sex, your name and nicknames, insects, leaves, tires, diseases, different medications and their effects; chemistry, books, movies, and on, and on, and on, and on, and on......and on. Think about how much we **each** know! Those things are only "the tip of the iceberg" because we are continuously moving and doing new things; therefore, everything around us is constantly changing and we are continuously comprehending everything as we adjust to those changes. We know and do a lot of things all at the same time.

ONLY spiritual beings created in the image and likeness of The Almighty God could possibly have that much unrestricted access to physical cognition, recognition, and physical memory recalls (when spiritually desired). We are very special spiritual existences living in defiled physical bodies (organic vehicles) which are subject to our spiritual wills. Our physical brains translate our spiritual thoughts into physical actions. We exist in an evil realm which is already sentenced to eternal damnation, and modern people worldwide are living in **more and more confusion** as more and more societies and cultures of people intentionally turn away from the knowledge of God in The Name of Jesus Christ. This is to be expected because we have already been told in The Holy Bible that we are born into a realm of the most demonic lies possible, and we physically develop in and around evil because the devil himself exists here.

Human beings are like children playing in the yard, but only SOME of us are listening to what "Dad" told us to do and not to do. We ALL have to go back inside at some point though, and we will each have to answer for our behaviors while we were outside. We are outside in the yard playing and a few of the children are reminding some of the other children about some of the things "Dad" said not to do. The inevitable responses towards those kids is, "Who do you think YOU are?!". "You guys are always trying to tell somebody else what to do!!". "You guys have done this before too, so shut-up!". "You think you are the only ones who are right, and you think you're better than everybody else!". "You make me sick!". "I hate you guys!", etc. Sound familiar?

Each of us has a free will and we can choose to believe whatever we want. We spiritually and physically *pay attention to everything* by being spiritually attentive to physical inputs coming in from our different physical senses (ears, tongue, eyes, skin, nose). Because we DO pay attention to everything in existence, we KNOW that spontaneous materialization of anything has never happened. Spontaneous materialization (if there was such a thing) would be the *sudden appearance* of random matter on its own *from nothing and for no reason at all.* For instance, a group of people would be sitting on a beach when suddenly a pecan pie with a baseball on it and some peanut butter and jelly on a rope inside of an unrecognizable "something" would appear out of nowhere and slide down an also spontaneously manifested bathroom wall in front of them. There would be no purpose for anything and unimaginable things would be happening whenever and wherever. Spontaneous materialization does not happen, and it never has. This universe is NOT spontaneous and we all KNOW that.

While I am riding a bicycle, 14 purple vacuum cleaners and a Musk Ox having a baby are not going to suddenly appear out of nowhere on a stack of something I've never seen before on the sidewalk in front of me. A ball of gooey slime the size of an SUV embedded with cheese and macaroni, a jet engine, and three Mako sharks are not going to suddenly appear on the 53rd floor of a skyscraper. These are examples of spontaneous materialization, and things do not spontaneously manifest themselves from nothing for no reason. Even if they **could** *possibly* do that (which is not possible), then how could any of those "things" be recognizable or useful to us (have any purpose) since they would be pointless, unplanned, meaningless matter? The truth is that nothing would make any sense to anybody.

When we make things, we imagine them first (note the root word, "image") and then we purposefully bring objects into physical existence by designing and manufacturing them. Physical materials are gathered and then manipulated to make things, and everything we physically make represents individual or collective spiritual thoughts borne from perceived physical needs or artistic desires. The fact is that **nothing** has **ever** happened for no reason and if the universe is a Godless spontaneous existence, then things would still be suddenly appearing for no reason at all. That would be reality, but we all know that is NOT the reality in which we exist. Everything is purposed; God is Reality.

Automobiles, planets, trains, boats, tissue, comets, staplers, water, crayons, shoes, nor anything else you can think of did not, and do not appear out of nowhere for no reason, and neither did this universe. That is absurd. Every element of every single physical bit of matter in existence has *very obviously* been *intelligently designed* with each part of each of those elements having its own functioning purpose. God is.

When people die, those of us who knew them may remember some physical characteristics about them, but we mostly remember their spirits. We remember some of the things they used to say and the way they used to say them. We remember the way they behaved, talked, thought, etc. We mostly remember spiritual things about them because we are each spirits operating in physical bodies. After people have died, we naturally say things like, "*His/Her* body was found over there in the bushes.", or "*The victim's* body was badly decomposed.", or "*Keith's* body was never found.", or "*His/Her* body was badly burned." and other similar expressions which all lead to the obvious question; "**Whose** body was it"? Those kinds of expressions naturally refer to the *fact* that a dead body is just a vehicle "a person" used to spiritually occupy, and that is the person we knew and remember.

Human beings can know a lot of information and while we are alive in this physical realm and in these physical bodies, we all wonder "why and how" about almost everything. We ask these questions because we inherently know there are purposes for every bit of matter in existence. God *purposefully* created everything, and He **wants** us to understand and appreciate His incredibly awesome physical creations. He gave us some beautifully excellent "tools" with which to do exactly that with, and numbers and words are two of those tools. Think about "numbers". What are "numbers"? Numbers are physical representations of spiritual amounts of the structure of this physical realm. God mathematically structured and balanced this entire physical realm and this is why it is numerically calculatable. This is why numbers work.

Unique marks represent different percentages of whatever they are being applied to, and different human beings in different cultures worldwide already know the same "percentages" or "amounts" each mark represents, even though the marks look completely different. This suggests without question that all human beings are already *spiritually* aware of each number's *amount or value*, and we only teach each other how to make and manipulate the marks which represent each amount so that we can understand God's creations and then communicate those amounts to each other. God gave us a "toolbox" of different numbers so that we can get things done. God is.

We teach each other numerical positions and orders. A "3" written in Japanese represents the same amount/portion as a "3" written in Hungarian, English, Ethiopian, Russian, or whatever else for example, and even though the representational marks look entirely different, we each already understand the amounts they represent. The "amounts" of each number become more and more tangible to each of us as we mature. Where did the "amount consistencies" of numbers come from? Did each kind of man come together in a worldwide "Numbers Meeting" and decide what the different amounts for each number would be? No. Think for yourselves because you are ultimately responsible for doing just that. The amount of each number was created by God to contain its specific amount of space, time, or calculatable portion of anything physical. God created this mathematically balanced universe **for** mankind, and He has given us tools like numbers to help us better understand it.

Spontaneity could not have "created" anything, and certainly not anything so stable that it is able to be predictably calculated! That's just stupid and makes no sense at all. People could **not** apply physical marks which represent amounts to any equation and get consistent results if numbers were not purposed. Consistency could not exist. "Amounts" would spontaneously change making any equation unreliable and therefore useless to us.

The *amount* of the number "7" for example, could not be the same everywhere if this existence was spontaneous because each amount of "7" would not retain any consistency.

10

Both the amount of the number and the physical number itself could spontaneously change at any given time. All numbers would spontaneously change since there would be no purpose for their existences and there could not be predictable consistencies to anything if there was no purpose for anything. If God did not create the values/amounts for numbers, then where else could the consistently structured amounts of each number have possibly come from? Yes; God did it.

Each human being is like one of the tiniest specks of microscopic bacteria compared to the Earth (let alone the universe), yet each human being understands so very much. We have indeed been created in the image and likeness of Almighty God, and we are as physically improbable as bits of bacteria on my left kneecap understanding where they are in proximity to the rest of my body as well as other intimate details about my body's physical composition and how my body operates. That microscopic bacteria on my kneecap would also understand that there are other human beings and how differently each one looks and acts, as well as a myriad of other incredibly accurate facts about its physically insignificant, yet spiritually aware existence. Each one of us is a special individual creation with divine purposes for existing. We are *spiritual images of **Almighty God*** contained in tiny, defiled physical bodies, and we each have access to God's Infinite Nature and Being through Jesus Christ by The Holy Spirit. There are *billions* of little images of Almighty God alive on this Earth in human bodies at any given point in time, so of course it takes this ridiculously expansive universe to contain us.

Human beings are spiritually incredible creations. When children are outside playing sports for example, they very clearly demonstrate that they already understand the complicated laws and applied dynamics of physics. Adults write formulas to communicate those same laws and dynamics using aforementioned numbers, but we are born already being able to understand the physics behind the numbers. Children playing football, baseball, soccer, and basketball, already understand the angles and velocities required to complete passes with those footballs, how to make accurate throws with baseballs, when to kick accurate shots into soccer nets while moving and avoiding defenders, and how hard to push a basketball towards the ground in order to make it come back up to the desired height so they can more easily bounce it again in whichever direction they desire. Think about the physics a person has to understand in order to make shots with a basketball, or to kick a ball into a goal while on the move. Think about the physics which must be understood to accurately throw football passes to receivers while they are running at different speeds and at different angles while being defended by other people.

Gravity, velocity, directions of travel, angles, the wind, small mounds or depressions in the ground, and many other considerations involving physics are all being quickly and correctly processed during actions which go into skillfully playing sports. Athletes do not have to be able to write down physics formulas and pass physics tests in classrooms before being able to be successful in sports; they already understand applied physics (some better than others). Mankind is special. We are incredible creations in physical bodies, and we inherently understand a lot more than we realize we do.

The very instant fertilization takes place between a man and a woman (a male sperm inserts into a female egg), a **male or female** *spirit of man* (Genesis 1:26-31 KJV) is "paired" with a physical human *body*. At that very first instant, the tiniest parts of physical cells are instructed on what to begin to make; a boy or a girl. The cells have to know what to start making, so they begin to divide accordingly and that union becomes *an independent, living, male or female* **soul** (Genesis 2:7 KJV) in this physical realm. A male or female body begins to grow and continues to grow before and after birth. That body will continue to grow and change throughout its physical existence, and if that body is not destroyed, diseased, or otherwise incapacitated, then that body will eventually grow old and it will not work like it used to work anymore. ALL bodies (every"body") eventually die. When that happens, the spirit in that body (you, me, and everyone else) is released from that body, and is then individually judged by God, through Jesus Christ concerning what he/she did while they were in that body. A physical body is a "vehicle" a spirit will be in for the entire time it physically exists.

Our brains are physical "computers" which translate spiritual thoughts into physical actions as directed by the individual spirit occupying that body. There is an ever-working double correlation between the spirit of each person, and each person's physical body, both positive and negative. That means that our bodies are physical and therefore sinful because they are literally made of defiled physical Earth (dirt), so our bodies naturally agree with the devil/evil. Our spirits are created in the image and likeness of The Holy and Righteous God, and that spirit of man naturally connects with The Holy Spirit which is of course; holy. My individual spirit (me, my soul, my personality existing in my body) has a free will, and I can **choose to** physically do and spiritually believe whatever I decide to physically do and spiritually believe. It behooves me to choose spiritual salvation (Jesus

Christ) from the inevitable eternal damnation of everything physical.

Spiritual information, thoughts, and expressed physical actions are recorded and stored in our brains in different ways and in different capacities depending on the individual. Consistently expressed behaviors eventually manifest recognizable (by others) "personalities". Personalities are patterns of people's behavioral choices and actions which are *almost* predictable. "Almost" predictable because we cannot reliably predict anybody else's behaviors, but we **can** have a pretty good idea about how other people will behave in different situations after we have been around them for a while. We say things like, "I know what Scott would have done if he had been here!", or "Tamara would never have stood for that! She would have …", or "You just wait until Selby gets back, he's going to….", etc. We can be correct about those things, but we can also be very wrong about predicting other people's behaviors and we end up saying things like, "I never thought Michele would do something like that!", or "I can't believe Mike said that to me!".

This is a spiritual existence and anyone who regularly competes in competitive sports understands that competitiveness goes far beyond just being physical. Almost every serious athlete is physically big, fast, strong, exceptionally coordinated, or otherwise gifted but always remember; there are *individual spirits* (personalities) controlling each of those bodies and when uniquely strong, confident, and ultra-competitive individual spirits play team sports and they are physically gifted, they strongly influence their teams' overall *spiritual expectations* of winning. This makes those teams much more difficult to beat, especially when those teams have more than one spiritually competitive and physically gifted athlete on them. When teams spiritually **expect to win** more than the teams they are competing against, then those teams almost always win unless they make too many physical mistakes during competitions. Gametime mistakes happen because nobody is perfect; we ALL make mistakes.

Spiritually dominant teams exist in every team sport worldwide and sports announcers commonly talk about the overall competitive spirits of different teams as well as the competitive spirits of the individual competitors making up those teams. The spiritual determination which these kinds of individual athletes compete with and compete against can be immense, and it is a beautiful thing to witness. There is much to be said about the spiritual realm when it comes to competitiveness in sports.

Our bodies are physical, and this means they are subject to physical realities such as time (which causes physical deteriorations), nutrition, hydration, injuries, temperature, gravity, disease, and other physical variables. A person's body can be perfectly healthy and otherwise able to live but **without its designated spirit in it**, that body is dead just like a parked car because it has no "driver". It has no spirit to operate it. Each of us is *spiritually* responsible for what our physical bodies do while we are in them, the exact same way we are responsible for what our automobiles do when we drive them. We will each be held spiritually accountable by Almighty God when our bodies die; and *every(body)* is going to die. Our bodies need to be maintained daily to work properly but regardless of what we do, the modern human **body** will no longer last more than 120 years in this physical realm. God said it will not (Genesis 6:3; KJV). There are billions of human beings alive on this planet at any given time right now, but not one person will live past the age of

120 years. There are people around the world who *claim* they are aware of folks over 120 years of age, yet NOT A SINGLE ONE OF THEM can be verified with documentation .... because they do not exist. They are ALL lies.

Why do human beings (along with **everything else** living in this physical realm) eventually die? Death cannot be explained outside of the Biblical Truth about death and why it exists (Genesis 2:17 KJV). Modern scientists giving physical explanations based on *probable causes* as to why someone has died, still does not answer the question; "Why?". Not one person out of trillions of people has lived past the age of 120 years since God said it, and naturally out of the billions of people alive right now, at least one person would be unusual (an outlier) and live longer than 120 years. It doesn't happen. We exist *within* a finite physical realm which has a definitive beginning (creation) and a definitive end (Judgement Day); therefore, **everything** existing *within* this finite realm (of course) HAS to have begun after the beginning and will definitely end either when, or before everything else ends. Everything manifested into this physical realm **must** end. The ultimate reason for the definitive end to all of this reality in which we exist is clearly explained in the King James version of the Chapter of Genesis, located in The Holy Bible, and one must read it for themselves to understand.

We do not know when God created this physical realm, nor do we know when it will end; but we certainly **know** that it **has begun**, and we also definitely **know** that **it will end** (Romans 14:11, 12; 2 Peter 3:10; Acts 17:31 KJV). When a person dies after *deciding not* to believe that Jesus Christ is God (rejecting and blaspheming The Holy Spirit), then eternal (spiritual) damnation awaits them. Every(**body**) is going to physically die, and then each person will be spiritually judged about how he/she operated his/her body while they were in them. Either they believed and tried to honor "God's Word", or they decided to blaspheme, curse, and reject Jesus Christ and continue to believe and behave as they pleased. There is eternal damnation for the latter decision. God is.

When born again Christians physically die, then we are *spiritually* instantly with Jesus Christ because *for God's children*, to be absent from the body is to be spiritually present with The Lord! Our *bodies* are physical though, and they remain here in this physical realm which is still subject to time (our bodies physically disintegrate). There is no such thing as "time" in the spirit realm.

Physical motion and time are physically connected. Time is a **finite realit**y which **only** exists in this physical realm and because time (as we know it) does not spiritually exist (in infinity), then there is no such thing as "time" to a dead person's spirit. Without us being in a human body, our individual spirits cannot access this physical realm anymore. After our bodies are dead, our personalities (individual spirits/souls) are permanently separated from this physical realm, and there are no human personalities (ghosts) existing in this physical realm without physical bodies. The ONLY spirits interacting with us in this physical realm without bodies are The Holy Spirit of God, God's angels, and the devil and his demons. Angels CAN be *physically* manifested into this physical realm (Hebrews 13:2 KJV), but demons spiritually attempt to convince people of lies and deceptions. Because we are constructed as we are (spirits in physical bodies), then sometimes we can physically perceive spiritual interactions in this physical realm. Both Holy AND demonic spirits *can* be invited into this physical realm by people, and the convicted liar (the devil) and his demons can also physically manifest apparitions, move things, and/or cause other kinds of physically perceivable interactions when we invite/allow them to do so.

The devil's desire is to kill us all. He IS pure evil and human beings represent God (pure righteousness), so if the devil *could* physically kill you, then you would already be dead. The devil CANNOT TELL THE TRUTH and he uses already existing thoughts and ideas in people's minds to help them misinterpret demonic apparitions (demons) as being "ghosts" of dead people and other mess like that. When people are receptive to that kind of evil confusion, then the devil gladly accepts their invitations. Again, there are no human ghosts roaming around this physical realm haunting people or places. Demonic, ghastly apparitions are only demons which people have unwittingly or otherwise spiritually invited through fear, confusion, or evil expectations. The devil (the anti-Christ) literally hates you to death, so choose Jesus The Risen Christ, because God is our salvation.

Our physical bodies manifest our individual souls' spiritually requested actions as well as they are physically able to do, and the physical conditions of each of our bodies greatly influences how we physically interact with everything else; especially other people. "Awareness"; or the phrase "to be aware of", literally means *"A person's sensitivity to the spirit realm in any given situation"*. Contemporary "worldly" definitions are worded differently because the world's "scientific professions" do not acknowledge the spirit realm at all.

Sensitivity to the spirit realm (awareness) varies significantly from person to person and when we are physically close to each other, our individual spirits interact with each other while we are also individually interacting with good and evil spirits. Most of the time we are aware of other people's spiritual levels of awareness (whether we are directly communicating with them or not) based on their physical "body language" and verbal expressions.

For example, if a sexually stimulated man in a nightclub is looking for a woman to have sex with that night and he begins a conversation with a group of women, then his spirit is continuously assessing each of their levels of spiritual awareness of his ultimate sexual intent based on their verbal responses and their physical reactions to his words and actions. He is spiritually looking for any sexual opportunities or vulnerabilities in any of the women which he can try to exploit. He will ask certain questions and say certain things so he can try to spiritually discern by their reactions if any of the women in the group are willingly receptive to his intent. We can physically interpret other people's spiritual moods and desires, and some people are more aware than others when it comes to these kinds of interpretations and interactions. Sometimes alcohol or other intoxicants can interfere with spiritual awareness levels, and this is how people can "sweet-talk" their ways into accomplishing sexual desires. Men and women end up wondering, "how in the world did I allow that to happen?!" later on.

If an angry-looking man wearing a long heavy trench-coat in the summertime walks into an auditorium full of people with his hands in his pockets, then at least a few people in that crowd will immediately spiritually assess him and be aware of his *possible* intentions. They will react to him based on that assessment and although he may just be a perfectly innocent man who came into the building to see what was going on, he may also be looking to violently hurt someone. Some people are not as spiritually aware as other people (regardless of the reasons), and this causes them to be more susceptible to becoming victims of otherwise avoidable crimes and negative situations. People's intentions, moods, desires, etc., whether good or evil, **can be** spiritually discerned. We spiritually discern other people's intentions while we're driving cars for example, and we become very angry when other drivers "intent"ionally disrespect us on the roads. Driving offers us a clear example of attentional awareness because we can perceive other people's levels of spiritual intents and situational awareness.

I was a teenager in a small economically depressed, racially segregated town in southern America. Back then whenever I would drive a car anywhere, I had to be spiritually aware of not only potential criminals, but also of racist law enforcement officers because at that time, there were many of them. Back then (circa 1980), law enforcement officers pretty much did whatever they wanted to do to black people, and I was stopped by law enforcement officers and had my license and registration checked without any probable cause more times than I should have been.

When I was 25 years old, I was falsely arrested and put in jail for no reason after I supposedly "fit the description" of a local rape suspect while I was in South Carolina. Had I been more spiritually aware at the time, I would have immediately gotten back into my car and left that area as soon as I saw the first young white police officer slowly cruise by and start hatefully looking at me. I was a young US Army officer (Second Lieutenant) at the time (not in uniform), and

I had gone to a gas station in Columbia, South Carolina in 1989 around 2am. I was going into the gas station when I noticed a patrol car drive by and suddenly slow down. I saw the officer look at me with a hateful look on his face, but I did not immediately spiritually discern the situation, so I continued into the store and talked and joked around with the store clerks. I eventually exited the store and started putting gas in my car when suddenly three police cars pulled into the station parking lot and as the officers (all of them white) got out of their cars, some of them pointed their guns at me and started yelling for me to hang up the gas pump and to keep my hands visible. The officers said they were arresting me on suspicion of rape (I "fit the description"). After putting me in the back seat of one of the cruisers, the officers began talking amongst themselves. The officers then told me they were arresting me for driving while my license was suspended (my driver's license was 100% valid at the time) and they ended up taking me to jail at around 3am where I stayed until about 11:00am the following morning.

I was not allowed to make a phone call during that entire time, and my mother was in a hotel room waiting for me to return from the gas station because we had gone to Ft. Jackson, South Carolina to see my younger brother (her son) graduate from US Army Basic Training. I had gone out that night to gas the car up ahead of time for the next day's drive back home after the ceremonies. The charges were later dropped and the case was dismissed after I wrote a letter to the Columbia, SC District Attorney (D.A.) explaining what had happened and threatening to sue them. All the money everything had cost me and even more was refunded to me and I never went to court, but I probably should have sued them anyway. That incident prompted me to want to become a police officer so I could better understand first-hand, how police officers get away with enforcing laws differently depending on which races they are dealing with. I became a police officer later that same year in North Carolina and served more than honorably for 6 years. I served and protected with honor, and I learned what I set out to learn about some of the ways racist law enforcement practices are in fact, still being perpetuated in America.

I have been criminally victimized by other people besides law enforcement personnel as well, and as a result I have developed into a more spiritually sensitive and discerning adult. Some years after my police career ended, I began driving semi-trailer trucks over the road for a major trucking company. While I was delivering a load to a small town in Louisiana, I suddenly passed an orange sign which said "No Trucks on Bridge Ahead – Bridge Under Construction/Repair". I couldn't see the bridge yet because the bridge was located around an upcoming curve. I therefore had to pull over as quickly as I could onto a dirt area on the right side of the road where many trucks had obviously turned around before. Because there was a sharp curve in the road immediately behind me, and the traffic coming from the other direction was relatively heavy (it was around 3:30pm), it would have been very unsafe for me to have attempted a U-turn. My 18-wheeler was fully loaded and my delivery site was less than two miles ahead on the right, but I could not cross the upcoming bridge so I was forced to make a U-turn. I did exactly what I should have done in that situation and called the local police department to ask for an officer to come and assist me with the traffic so I could safely turn my tractor-trailer around.

From the very second the young white officer got out of his car and put on his shades like he was "the man", I

22

discerned his spirit and had a feeling he was not going to be too willing to "protect and serve" MY needs. Sure enough, as soon as the officer got to my truck and noticed that I was a black man, he immediately reacted by putting his hands on his hips like he was tough, and then asked me what I needed. I knew I was going to have to maintain complete spiritual control over my physical desires to confront this already disrespectful man because I didn't want to go to jail or get shot by this idiot for no reason. I explained the situation to the officer and he agreed with everything I said and then proceeded to stop the traffic behind me so I could get turned around.

After I turned around and began to travel in the opposite direction, he too turned around and drove behind me for about two blocks and then turned on his lights and sirens to stop me. He had obviously called for backup because another officer soon appeared and both cars had blue lights flashing. I pulled my truck into a shopping center parking lot and both of the young white officers approached my truck walking like they were John Wayne. They asked me to step out of the truck and they checked all of my paperwork (which was 100% correct and updated). I was not spiritually surprised at all when the officer started writing me a ticket after making several unnecessarily smart-mouthed remarks. When I asked him why in the world he was writing me a ticket, he said verbatim, "I'm tired of trucks doing that!". "Doing what?", I replied. "Turning around right there like that!", he said. "Oh and so you're going to start writing tickets with me now?!", I asked. He never made eye contact with me, and didn't say anything else. He just tore the ticket out and handed it to me. To say the least, I was not happy with that idiot at all.

I had already perceived his contentious spirit long before he wrote me that ticket, so I kept myself calm the entire time knowing full well that this ticket would have zero merit in court. I told that stupid officer that the signs were posted way too late for any truck to have done anything other than what I had done, and that this was the reason trucks "kept doing that". Of course, the ticket was thrown out of court before the court date.

My spiritual perceptions allowed me to remain in control of my physical actions that day because I had been on the receiving end of racists officers before, and had already been a police officer myself. I was also a US Army combat veteran by that time and I had a perfectly clean driving record. I knew that I had done what I was supposed to have legally done in that situation, yet here was this idiot; writing me a ticket. After the officers left, I drove my truck back down the exact same route I had taken and filmed everything to show that the warning signs were ridiculously inadequate. I was ready to go to court with the film and my written summation of what had been said and done, but the case never made it that far. Spiritual awareness is critically important to how we physically respond in situations and circumstances, and the more spiritually aware we are of each other, the more effectively we can handle and even avoid negative situations and circumstances.

Sensitivity to the spirit realm is awareness, and the level of each person's spiritual awareness is lessened by physical attentional activities. Physical attentional activities are indicators of what we call *consciousness*, and a person is deemed to be conscious when they continuously display intentional acts of directing one or more of their senses to gather information from particular areas of interest (i.e., they are intentionally looking at something, listening to something, touching or smelling something, etc.).

We sometimes intensify our physical senses by concentrating them on selected areas of interests, and some physical indicators of sensory intensifications are squinting to see better, closing our eyes to hear better, or making facial expressions as we concentrate on something. The *ability to pay attention* is therefore an indicator of physical consciousness, and we each remember all kinds of information we have paid attention to while we have been conscious during our lifetimes.

During times of unconsciousness (diminished physical attentional activities) such as sleeping, being knocked out, comatose conditions, etc., our awareness of the spirit realm increases and after we have regained full physical consciousness, it is difficult to put those spiritual interactions into words. Some aspects of those interactions are sometimes remembered however, and people speak of dreams, visions, lights, and/or other experiences. The spiritual realm and the physical realm are two **completely different** realms and although the two realms are combined in life forms in this physical realm, they are yet completely different. Our spirits do not roam freely without a body in this physical realm any more than our physical bodies can roam freely in the spirit realm. Our spirits **must** remain **in** our physical bodies in order for us to be able to experience this physical realm.

We are individual human spirits continually in contact with The Holy Spirit as well as demonic spirits as we operate *through* our physical bodies, and whether or not we individually accept God (The Holy Spirit) in The Name of Jesus Christ is a free-will decision we must each make before our bodies die; which they will. This entire physical realm is an atmosphere of spiritual interactions through organic matter. For example, we can be spiritually aware of someone else's physical presence in places without seeing, hearing, or otherwise *physically* sensing them. People commonly say things like, "I had a feeling someone was over there...", or "I knew somebody was in here.", or "I felt like someone was watching me", etc. Sometimes we look in particular directions for no specific reasons and then find ourselves making direct eye contact with someone else. Those are not coincidences. This is a spiritual existence.

I drove a full-sized conversion van with very dark tinted windows (limousine tint) all the way around with a curtain behind the front seats when I went back to college as an adult. I would inevitably have to park near particularly busy sidewalks on campus, and I would sit at a table in the back of my van a lot between classes. I observed thousands of college students and others continuously walking by the van day after day. My classes were at various times and places, so I would park wherever I could park on campus in different places. My van was just another parked car out of the thousands of parked cars all over the campus, and if the people walking by did not already know I was in one of the seats in the back of my van, there is no way they could have known. I knew for a fact that people could not have been seeing me from any perspective up and down the entire length of those sidewalks because I would get out and check the van at various times during the day to make sure that I could not have been being seen through the windows.

As I sat in the back of that van next to those different sidewalks day after day, so many different people would make direct and extended eye contact with me in the back of

26

that van that I had to get out of the van on several occasions to check and make sure that they were not in fact seeing me. It happened so often I began to think, "Well, even if they DO somehow know that I am in this van, they still have no way of knowing *where* I am back here, so why do so many people keep looking directly at me?!" I KNEW that they could not have been physically seeing me. All those different people making direct extended eye contact with me through that limousine tinted glass were undoubtedly spiritually sensing my presence. I know that my observations were not "traditionally scientific", but a significant number of random people made direct and extended eye contact with me day after day regardless of where I would park and then position myself in the back of that van. I came to the 100% conclusion that people were indeed spiritually aware of my presence in the back of that van because how else could all those random folks have been unknowingly looking directly into my eyes? They did not consciously know that they were looking at me, but they were. We are spirits in physical bodies for sure, and we are spiritually aware of each other.

Sleep is an inevitable function of the physical body because the body needs to regularly rest to repair its physical components so that it can operate normally the next time it is conscious. Almost every day, we (our individual souls) position our individual bodies somewhere safe so we can intentionally diminish our physical attentional activities to the point that physical relaxation is possible and we go to sleep (we allow our bodies to go into an unconscious state). While someone is sleeping, the personality/spirit in that body remains the same; you are still who you are but now there are greatly diminished physical attentional activities to impede your spiritual interactions. Our spirits cannot completely leave our bodies while we are sleeping or our bodies will die, so the freedom of the spirit is still limited by the sleeping body because the physical condition of our bodies must be continually "manned". This is evidenced by a sleeping person's awareness and recognition of temperature changes, uncomfortable body positions, unusual or unexpected sounds and movements, bathroom needs, etc.

Sometimes when we sleep, spiritual interactions *physically* stimulate us enough that "dreams" result. Dreams are what we can physically remember about those spiritual interactions, and spiritual interactions are not always accurately remembered after a person wakes up. We already know that most people do not often describe things they have physically (consciously) witnessed as accurately as it seems like they would, so we can infer with confidence that people's descriptions of spiritual interactions are probably even less accurate. In other words when people say what they dreamed about, they are undoubtedly leaving out and distorting all kinds of information. This is why dreams seem silly or don't make chronological sense to us most of the time. We seem to remember each dream like a series of still photographs immediately after we wake up, and we then consciously fill in the "gaps" between the "stills" as we attempt to verbalize the dreams so as to make rational stories from them. The "stills" fade from our conscious memories a short time later and we end up forgetting about most dreams altogether. Dreams sometimes physically stimulate brain neurons and cause physical reactions to occur, and if most of us could have been observed while we were having those kinds of physically interactive dreams, we were probably swinging, smiling, masturbating, changing facial expressions, or expressing some other form of physical activity.

When these kinds of physical activities occur during dreams, it *seems like* those dreams would be easier to remember because physical neurons in the brain relating to those physical activities were stimulated the same way they would have been stimulated had we been conscious. This doesn't seem to be the case however, and it is one of the myriad of interesting things about our spirit/body combinations. People who "sleep-walk" for example, do not normally remember walking around while they were sleeping, but the exact same neurons, muscular cells, sight pathways, etc., which are stimulated while they are conscious and walking around, are obviously being stimulated while they are sleep-walking (or else they would not be walking around). We are the same personality (spirit) in dreams as we are when we are conscious, so of course we react to situations and circumstances in dreams the same way we would react if we were conscious. Your spirit (personality) residing in your body does not change just because your physical body is unconscious, so you do not become "someone else" while you are sleeping, drugged out, or otherwise incapacitated.

Some people say they do not believe there is a spiritual realm, but because every human being is an individual **spirit** in an individual body, those *exact same people* say things like, "**I** have a headache.", or "**My** knee hurts." Those are declarations which express possession, and possession of anything **requires** two different existences. There has to be "something" which has "something else", and those are two different things. There absolutely **HAS** to be a *separate assessment* of a person's own body in order for that same person to be able to make **any evaluations about themselves** such as, *"my* knee hurts", or "*I have* a headache". Whose knee is it? Whose head is it which has that pain? Who recognizes

29

that "their" knee or head is not functioning correctly? It is the spirit *in* that body who recognizes that something is wrong with its body. "**You**" are in control of what "**your**" body does and every(**body**) is going to die. "You" will not die when your body does, but you **will** be held accountable for how you spiritually directed your body to operate while you were in it. Every living human being in existence will be judged when their body ceases to live.

When there is a problem with a vehicle someone is driving, the driver (the "spirit" in that vehicle) says for example, "**I have a flat tire.**", or "**My** battery is getting weak", or "**My** window won't go down", or whatever the problem is. Drivers of cars and the cars themselves are two completely different things the same way human spirits and human bodies are different. When we say things like, "**My** arm hurts.", or "**My** finger is broken.", those are indicators and evidences of that relationship.

Regardless of whether drivers are speeding and running red lights, or if drivers are properly obeying the written rules of the roads; drivers are 100% accountable for how they direct their cars to operate while they are in them, and the exact same thing is true about human beings. Make sure you pay attention to your "road rages" (how you treat other people). Also, be careful about where you "park your car" because others may notice "your car" parked in places they should probably not have been parked (smile). That's all I will say about that….

The spirits of human beings are practically non-existent to modern scientists and there is no justifiable explanation as to why. It is obvious that the devil has modern scientists confused and in denial. The reality of the human spirit is consistently demonstrated in this life and it deserves to be acknowledged and professionally investigated far more than it is in modern science. For example, individual human spirits integrate into anything physical we can get into and control; especially mobile objects. We eventually begin to "feel" the parameters and edges of whatever it is we are physically controlling because we spiritually integrate into objects more and more the longer we stay in them. Our personal cars are perfect examples of this. We get more and more "used to" our personal cars, and we can eventually handle almost any road situation without hitting anything because we **know and can feel** where the physical edges of that vehicle are without having to get out and look at it.

If a very good driver gets behind the wheel of a much larger vehicle for the first time, they will not be able to handle that large vehicle in tight situations as well as a good (or even below average) driver who has driven that same vehicle many times before. That being said, some people spiritually integrate into physical objects exceptionally quickly while for some others, the entire integration process is very challenging. Integrational time frames vary widely between people

The spiritual integration process also occurs when amputees receive inanimate artificial limbs. People eventually spiritually integrate into those "new" parts and learn to control them better and better the longer they integrate into them. Our spirits can also integrate into organic tissue, and because of this we can successfully transplant all kinds of body parts and limbs from certain (agreeable) bodies into and onto other living bodies. Also, because the spiritual and physical realms are completely separate and different, even when transplants take place, people's personalities (spirits) always remain the same even after they have received organic transplantations (parts from another body). Our bodies are only physical

31

vehicles we spiritually use so that we can exist in this physical realm. Organic, human transplantations such as heart and kidney transplants are comparable to removing carburetors or oil filters from one car's engine and placing them onto another agreeable vehicle's engine. This has nothing to do with the "drivers" (spirits) of either of those "vehicles", but has everything to do with their "physical machines" (bodies).

When we get "used to" driving any kind of vehicle (regardless of size, type, mission, etc.), that literally means that we have mostly completed a spiritual integration into that vehicle. Spiritual integrations take place at different rates and at different quality levels for each person, and these differences between people are easily observable when people learn to drive cars for example. Eventually people "learn" how far away an opposite bumper is from other objects without having to get out of the car to look to see how close things are (new drivers must do this). The longer we control any mobile object the more we spiritually integrate into the parameters of that object; so much so, that we can back extremely large vehicles into tight spaces without hitting anything. We can also "safely" drive large trucks on narrow cliff roads and land large airplanes on tiny runways without crashing. The spirits of human beings can do all kinds of awesome things and human spirits deserve to be scientifically acknowledged.

When we were children, each one of us continuously integrated into our bodies as they were growing the same way we now integrate into cars, trucks, planes, ships, and anything else. When experienced Boeing 747 "Jumbo Jet" pilots are taxiing on tarmacs around other aircraft for example, they do not have to continuously look at their wingtips to make sure they are not going to make contact with other aircraft parked nearby (as brand new pilots training on that same aircraft have to do). They know exactly where those wingtips are. I have often wondered if there is a physical size limit to our spiritual integrations because there does not seem to be. Mining trucks, or "haul trucks" as they are known in the mining industry, are so incredibly large that it is hard to imagine that one person can safely operate most of those huge trucks without crashing into all kinds of things, but individual people operate those trucks every day all over the world without incidents. Mining haul-truck drivers have integrated into those oversized vehicles so much so that they "feel" and "know" exactly where the truck's rear tire on the opposite side from them is located, and they can accurately determine by "feel" that wheel's status, position, angle, etc. The drivers do not have to get out of the truck and look at it as I would absolutely have to do right now, because I am not a haul truck driver. Good operators of extremely large equipment are uniquely talented at spiritually integrating into mechanical objects, and though we can all spiritually integrate into things, some people do not integrate as well as others and their integrations are not very reliable. This is evidenced by the myriad of unsafe, barely integrated, dangerous drivers out here on these public roads (regardless of how long they have been driving); thank God for law enforcement officers!

"Pay attention!" What do we mean when we say to someone else, "Pay attention!"? We say that to someone else because we want them to immediately spiritually refocus their physical senses onto whatever or wherever it is we desire. The personality inside that body makes the decision to either redirect their senses to wherever it is we want them to, or they can refuse to do so. Each of us spiritually controls where we physically focus our senses, and what we pay attention to.

Our attentional processes can; however, be *involuntarily refocused* by external stimuli such as unexpected loud noises or sudden occurrences. In such situations, our bodies respond faster than our spirits can direct them to react, and these are known as orientation responses. For instance, if someone unexpectedly sets off a loud firecracker near your location right now, then your body would most likely initially react by jumping and looking before your spirit could regain conscious control of your attentional processes. This is commonly observed in camera footage from various places when unexpected gunshots or other sudden loud noises occur in crowded areas. Most people turn towards where they think the sounds are coming from, and then hesitate (some longer than others) before reacting in controlled manners. In the firecracker example before the firecracker went off, your spirit and body were focused on whatever it was you were doing and in the first instant after the blast, your physical senses were involuntarily reoriented to the direction of the noise and light. Your physical brain will not immediately decipher the instant deluge of physical information from your different senses, and nothing will make sense to you until you are able to spiritually regain control of your attentional processes (regain functional consciousness). Depending on any resulting physical injuries from the incident and the personalities of the individuals involved, regaining functional consciousness may take anywhere from about a half second to a much longer time. This temporary juxtaposition of the spirit and body is academically referred to as shock, and the differences in reintegration times ("coming back to your senses") happen for various reasons including those mentioned above, and age, physical condition, previous experiences, spiritual "intestinal fortitude", and also some other factors which I will discuss in detail in the next paragraph.

"Shock" is occurring when the spirit is trying to physiologically reconnect with the body after an unexpected refocusing incident. Whatever a person immediately heard, saw, felt, smelled, etc. (in this case, an unexpected firecracker explosion), is initially non-sensible to their brain, especially if it is outside of the normal parameters of occurrences for them. A person who works in a place where firecrackers go off unexpectedly all the time would most likely have less of an orientation and shock response to a firecracker unexpectedly exploding when they are somewhere else.

Our brains instantly attempt to physically rationalize sudden unexpected incidents while simultaneously attempting to manage our bodies' adrenal and physical responses. Sudden floods of simultaneous, sensual inputs can sometimes be too much for the brain to instantly process (identify/manage) and when this happens, our spirits cannot use the normal neural pathways in the brain because sudden "traffic jams" have occurred. There is too much information suddenly coming in for the brain to process, and the information needing to be processed gets clogged up. Most of the time (depending on the severity of the shock) the brain will relatively quickly settle down again and start processing information. The spirit can eventually re-access the normal neural pathways and people begin to act normally again. This happens very quickly for some people regardless of the severity of the stimulating incident but for some others, a return to normalization takes much longer.

People can be involved in or witness a traumatic incident and then afterwards not be able to describe what happened, even though they may appear to be spiritually experiencing the incident over again. They are in a much longer period of shock and their spirits have yet to fully physically reintegrate. The "reintegration process" (shock dissipation) also depends on the depth of spiritual control a person already has over their physical body before the incident took place. For example, a person who has been in the vicinity of dead human bodies on regular occasions would be far less likely to go into shock if they were unexpectedly exposed to a dead person's body; whereas a person who has never seen a dead body before would be more likely to go into shock if they were in that same situation. Only "more likely" because human beings are complex integrations of spirits and bodies, and each of us can react differently than expected in any given situation.

After someone has been in shock and is obviously beginning to recover, we say that he or she is "coming back their senses." Who is coming back? Who is it that went away from using their physical senses? It is the spiritual personality which occupies that body who is coming back, and although our spirits may immediately fully recognize what is going on during involuntary refocusing incidents, our physical brains are finite and sometimes become overwhelmed and cannot immediately process what is physically happening. We are spiritual beings operating in a physical realm in these awesome machines called human bodies, which translate our spiritual desires into physical actions. God created something magnificently incredible when He created human beings..... just look around at what we have done.

We are each a human spirit created in the image of Pure Righteousness, contained in physically evil human bodies (Psalms 51:5; KJV). There is a natural positive correlation between the *human spirit* and The Holy Spirit, and a natural negative correlation between the human body and The Holy

Spirit. There is also a natural *positive* correlation between the **human body** and demonic spirits because our bodies are literally made of condemned physical matter (dirt from the Earth), and demonic spirits are sentenced to the same condemnation as the physical Earth. *Everything physical* and the devil and his demons are already sentenced to eternal damnation; this includes our bodies. Remember; we are physically born into sin and shaped in iniquity, and we exist in an atmosphere where spiritual *and* physical sin exists. This is why we have to be "saved". This is what spiritual salvation in The Name of Jesus Christ is all about.

Every conscious person at any given point in time is consistently manifesting behaviors influenced by percentage combinations of good and evil, and physical and spiritual variables. Two of the most important **physical variables** are the contemporary physical environment, and the physical health of an individual. The physical ability to manifest spiritually intended behaviors is different in each body due to genetics, bodily injuries, different sicknesses, etc. **Spiritual variables** include encouraging and discouraging influential spirits. *Influential spirits* are either Holy (righteous), or demonic (evil), and each person makes final determinations as to which behaviors they ultimately decide to express. We each get "set" in our ways as we form our personalities, and our decisions eventually form our personalities. Sometimes reprobation occurs, and I will discuss reprobation later in Chapter (3).

We are spiritual beings experiencing this physical realm *through* physical bodies, and if we can intentionally pay attention to anything physical with any of our senses then we are alive and conscious, and our bodies are at least somewhat functional. Sometimes when people's bodies have been physically damaged, their spirits are not able to override the physical conditions of their bodies and they can *only try* to physically express themselves. This is like someone driving a malfunctioning vehicle on the highway. If that vehicle is operating slowly because of those malfunctions, then the driver of that vehicle may **intend** to signal and function just as quickly as others do, but the driver's intentions are severely restricted because of the damaged vehicle they are in. There is *no problem* with the driver, but the physical car is reacting slower to his/her inputs the same way a physically challenged person's body reacts more slowly (if at all) to their spiritual inputs. The spiritual people in those bodies are the same as everyone else, but their "vehicles" are damaged and not functioning properly. Our bodies are "vehicles" we get around in and they require spiritual energy to operate just as vehicles require the energy of a driver.

The manifestation of people's spiritual desires through their physical bodies is greatly influenced by **at least** *three major factors:*
    - The *physical condition* of the body's senses (eyes, ears, skin condition, etc.)
    - The body's *contemporary location/situation* (Am I in physical danger? Do I need to look, listen, run, etc.?)
    - Personal *spiritual desires* (intentionally concentrating and listening, or just lustfully *looking* at him/her rather than *listening* to what he/she is saying).

There are more factors which influence behaviors, but these are three of the main ones.

The exact same amount of spiritual energy (the spirit of man) exists in every living human being from birth, but that spiritual energy is manifested through each physical body differently because of each body's physical capabilities due to physical genetics. The amount of spiritual energy inhabiting each living body (the spirit of man) does not change throughout a human life cycle, but our physical bodies do. The abilities of each human body are genetically different and over our lifetimes, those abilities gradually increase as we mature and get bigger and stronger. Physical abilities reach a plateau at their highest levels when we reach our "athletic primes" and from then on, our physical abilities lessen more and more as we progressively age. Physical abilities naturally deteriorate with the passage of time because of age, genetics, exercise, amounts of water and different foods we have consumed over the years, atmospheric compositions, injuries, etc.

Our athletic/energetic prime-times seem to occur somewhere between the ages of 19 and 41 years, and the duration of this prime athletic/energetic period for each person depends heavily on those previously mentioned *physical* variables such as genetics, exercise, cumulative food and water intakes, etc. There are of course, people who are unusually energetic before and after these ages, but most people fall within this age range. As we physically grow and develop, our physical bodies require more and more spiritual energy to operate. While we are children, the amount of spiritual energy available to us is more than enough to operate our little physical bodies. We are born with enough spiritual energy to power an adult body, and this is why little bodies fall asleep so much; they are spiritually "overpowered" so to speak. Infants become physically exhausted quickly and sleep often, and toddlers literally collapse in place. The amount of spiritual energy operating in them physically "burns them out" and parents of toddlers, daycare workers, teachers, and others who are around young children can attest to this. Young children need naps because their little bodies get burned out from having too much energy, and older people get tired and need more naps because their bodies are progressively requiring more and more spiritual energy to function (because older cells and genetic functions require more spiritual energy to operate). God knew what He was doing when He created our spirits and made our bodies.

After the spiritual/physical equilibrium period (prime time) has passed, staying fully alert and energized all day long becomes more and more of a physical challenge the more we age. We attempt to *physically* recharge ourselves as we age with caffeine drinks and other physical stimulants because they help our bodies manifest spiritually desired behaviors quicker and for longer periods of time. We can still jump around, aggressively dance, run, play, etc., but our desires to be active like that lessen more and more because our bodies now need that same spiritual energy for basic physical operations. Our cells require more and more energy to operate because they are older and are processing information more slowly. This is kind of like older batteries wearing down in powered devices; the cells require more energy to work like they used to. All living things slow down as they age after their equilibrium period. Of course physical bodies (just like everything else) age, and extra activities (like the ones mentioned above) become unnecessary energy-burning operations which eventually require us to spiritually change our physical behavioral priorities. This change is needed because our bodies progressively become physically weaker and we are physically prone to more injuries and illnesses. We indeed need to be less physical. As our bodies age, they can sometimes manifest different behaviors than the residing spirit intends to manifest because of physical deteriorations such as Alzheimer's Disease, broken hips and bones, Dementia, etc. During stages of brain deteriorations due to age-related diseases or injuries, a person may intend to speak someone's name they have known all their lives for example, but they spiritually realize they cannot remember that name they know they know. The resulting frustrations in people going through this can be physically perceived and they can in fact tell you that they should be able to remember that name. This is verification that there is someone inside that body who recognizes it is deteriorating.

Older people spiritually recognize for themselves how they are physically changing and deteriorating, and sometimes people are embarrassed when these kinds of things start happening to them. Their spirits know that their physical brains used to store that information, and they are spiritually "looking" for it. It must be spiritually frustrating to realize that your physical brain cells are irrevocably deteriorating and again, we can physically see frustrations over these kinds of things taking place in people as they become more and more elderly.

There is a spiritual realm and there is a physical realm, and **only** in human beings is this combination manifested as self-conscious, self-aware individuals who are each spiritually aware of (sensitive to) good and evil spirits through a physical body. We are conscious spirits in temporary physical bodies in a temporary physical realm, and physical consciousness **IS** attentional awareness.

Attentional Awareness is *an individual spirit's ability to use its physical body's senses.* God incredibly engineered our

41

genetically constructed works of unmatched physiological art (our bodies) with sensory intakes, and in Chapter (2); "GENETICS; A WAY TO UNDERSTAND", I will talk more about the AWESOME job God did when He created humanity….. Hallelujah!!

(CHAPTER TWO)
GENETICS; A WAY TO UNDERSTAND

God has given us the tools of numbers and words to help us better understand everything; animals use neither. In this chapter I will use some of our abilities to communicate to help explain genetics by making some direct comparisons.

Modern scientists have discovered that life forms are constructed from different combinations of these (so far) identified nucleotides in each species' DNA (Deoxyribonucleic Acid): Adenine (A), Cytosine (C), Guanine (G), and Thiamine (T). The problem is that modern scientists *do not want* to acknowledge the *obvious fact* that ONLY The Almighty God could have created these purposely functioning, practically innumerable nucleotides which physically manifest each characteristic of each life form. GOD IS ETERNAL BRILLIANCE! God created every manifestation in existence, and we only **discover and study** already existing micro-macro biological and micro-macro inanimate systems via our scientific processes.

Writing is a physical ability we use to intentionally communicate with each other by using different-looking marks which are interpreted by anyone who can read and understand that particular language. Each mark is called a letter, and groups of different letters are intentionally placed together in particular orders next to each other to form different words. Each physical word conveys spiritual meanings and when we place words next to each other in what we call sentences, we can communicate with each other in very deep and complex ways.

Words are physical "vehicles" which transport spiritual ideas (thoughts). Thoughts then produce emotions which act as catalysts for physical behaviors (Holy or demonic). Emotions do not cause behaviors, but they highly influence the behavioral choices we continuously make. Because words have this kind of power, we need to be mindful of the words we listen to, read, speak, or otherwise expose ourselves to. This is critically important for many reasons. Just as we should eat good, healthy foods for our **physical** bodies to remain strong, we also need to listen to and read good, healthy spiritual "food" in order for our **spirits** to remain strong and healthy. The Holy Word of God is packed with every bit of the healthiest spiritual nutrition in existence!

Words are immensely powerful (Proverbs 18:21 KJV). Words carry spiritual information, and one day a husband wrote something on a piece of paper and gave it to his wife as they sat together on a bench laughing, talking, and obviously having a nice time. She took the paper from him and continued to talk to him for a little while before she read what was on the paper. After she read what was written on the paper she became noticeably hurt and emotionally angry all at the same time. She left the area crying.

Her husband only handed her a small piece of paper, but it was clear that he'd handed her a lot more than that. He gave her something which was able to affect her spiritual and emotional being. There were some "vehicles" on that piece of paper which transported spiritual ideas which powerfully changed her emotional status. The words stimulated her emotions which are now about to influence her behavioral actions. The husband had written the following on that piece of paper:

> *"It's true, I lied to you. I really DID have sex with your mother and yes… that really WAS me leaving her home that night you've always asked me about. I have been lying to you because I cannot stand the sight of you*

anymore. Me and your mother are in love and we have been for a while now…. After I divorce you, I plan to marry your mother, and by the time we get back home today, the moving company should already have my things loaded. Goodbye!"

Just as we combine individual letters in words and sentences to express our intended meanings, God has combined the individual nucleotides (Adenine (A), Cytosine (C), Guanine (G), and Thiamine (T)) in organic DNA strands to express His intended meanings. The nucleotides in the DNA strands of living organisms have properties comparable to vowels and consonants, and "long and short" sounds in individual letters of different languages. Nucleotides can also have silent or blended properties and for all we know, they could also be abbreviated or made into acronyms deciphered by certain cells because of the myriad of mysterious genetic communicational sequences which are obviously taking place.

There are only 26 letters available to us in the English language, yet we can make all kinds of specific words with precise, independent meanings because of the many variables letters have. God created us to be literate and our abilities to read and write provide us opportunities to understand some of the complexities of organic genetics. When we write, *each letter* in each word has the potential to be powerfully influential in many ways, and there can be major differences in overall expressions if only a few letters in a few thousand words are different in specific places. The exact same thing is true in genetics. For example, if one book has "could" and another has "couldn't" in only one pivotal place, or "his" instead of "hers", or "died" instead of "did", etc., then the overall expressions of each of those books would be significantly altered in various ways and again, the same thing is true in genetics. Organic bodies are literally "constructed" during the birth process and the positions of each tiny genetic nucleotide within those chains can be powerfully influential to the manifestation of the final organism. The position of each nucleotide in each DNA chain helps determine different physical manifestations in each member of each species making them each different from each other while still maintaining that particular species. For example, there are many different-looking puppies from a single litter of puppies, but they are all still dogs. If each of the different-looking dogs lives long enough to reproduce, what will every single one of them reproduce? They will reproduce more litters of different looking dogs and the same thing is true for every organic species in existence. None of the puppies born to any of those dogs will ever be naturally selected to be leopards, and even though two of the dogs may have been born without back legs, or two human babies may be born without arms or legs, each of those organisms are STILL what they are; dogs and human beings. They are not changing into another species! If future atheists were to find the remains of those particular abnormal dog and human bodies, they would undoubtedly proudly claim that they had found the remains of two transitional species and then present them to the world as evolutionary transitions.

Species do not change and they never have. Because atheists have found no transitional species (species in the process of changing their DNA into another species), they are now falsely claiming that every living organism is currently in the process of transitioning into something else. They are claiming this foolishness because in spite of the ongoing lies, they have not been able to identify a single half-anything species, nor show that there has ever been such a thing; because there has not been. Please, do not believe all these rampantly blatant, demonic lies! There is no evolution. Even though some species' DNA chains are very similar, we KNOW that DNA does not spontaneously change, and that different but similar animal species do not **NATURALLY** interbreed and reproduce, regardless of how similar they may look, sound, move, smell, etc.

"Martin did like everyone else." is significantly different from a sentence stating that "Martin died like everyone else." The first sentence means that a lot of people were doing something and Martin did the same thing everybody else was doing, while the second sentence communicates an entirely different meaning. It means that everybody is dead including Martin. There is only *one letter* which is different between the two sentences and if one of these sentences was in one book and the other sentence was in another book, then those books would express significantly different meanings and would not be the same even though they are both still books. Remember, that powerful difference would be caused by only one letter out of many thousands in a book. Again, genetics are the exact same way.

Libraries all over the world are full of different looking books and they are different because the letters within each book are positioned differently. Magazines and newspapers also utilize the exact same letters and words, but they are not books and they never will change into books just because they contain the same letters. We made books and magazines to be and to remain as they are, so books and magazines turning into each other is just as foolish as Chimpanzees changing into human beings. The exact same "letters" may occur often in books all over the world and each of those letters has the potential to be absolutely critical to the entire meaning of each book (as in the previous "Martin" example). Those letters may also be silent, long, short, or almost insignificant in those books, and the same letters are used in magazines, newspapers, etc., the same way the same genetic nucleotides are used in alligators, potatoes, dogs, worms, and all kinds of other organic DNA chains. Each letter's (nucleotide's) influence can range from being functionally insignificant to being absolutely critical depending on its location in a "word". None of this; however, has anything at all to do with one species being naturally selected to spontaneously change into another species any more than a book would spontaneously change into a magazine or newspaper because they are using the same letters.

The nucleotides Adenine (A), Cytosine (C), Guanine (G), and Thiamine (T), obviously possess multi-variable qualities which we can directly compare to alphabetic letters, but right now we do not understand exactly how and when those qualities are expressed. We investigate genetics and we can physically manipulate genes, chromosomes, nucleotides, etc., but that does not mean that we should do so in *immoral, reckless and inconsiderate* manners. Genetic research combining animal genes from different species is producing results that "don't make sense" because we are trying to combine two different "languages" using different "letters" which have multiple variables we do not understand at all. The words and sentences do not make sense so the "manifested meanings" are not making much sense.

There is nothing wrong with conducting science (1 Timothy 6:20-21). God ***intends*** for us to investigate His AWESOME creations, but ***definitely not*** with the modern motivations **TO TRY** and disprove The Word of God. God created everything just like the Holy Bible says God did, and THAT is **The Only Truth** there is concerning this existence. Science in every single genre continually shows us with 100% certainty that God created everything (Colossians 1:16), and there is absolutely no justifiable reason to believe otherwise. Hellfire awaits those who choose to blaspheme God.

Genetic studies show that our bodies are incredible machines designed with the same biological concepts and mechanisms as a lot of other organic creations in this physical existence, and sometimes there are only small genetic differences (nucleotides in DNA) between different species. God in His infinite wisdom, designed "functional genes" which exist amongst the trillions of other genetic materials. Functional genes along with other responsibilities, turn other genes on and off at perfect times during development (formation in the womb) and this causes those genes to instruct cells to make each part of the individual organism they are forming. These instructions are communicated in perfect sequential order to physically produce each form of life. This literally makes the foolish idea of spontaneous "natural selection" physically impossible, and all natural sciences verify that 100%. There is no evolution and if there is, who is doing all this "naturally selecting"?

Human beings are genetic just like mice, pigs, chimpanzees, and other biological creatures, but this in no way means that we evolved from any other animal after going through some sort of imaginary, spontaneous process of natural selection. That is as ridiculous as houseflies in my house "knowing" that the box of cereal on my refrigerator spontaneously evolved from a smaller cardboard box in my garage because they look similar and are constructed with some of the same materials.

The boxes may have been designed by the same person in the same factory using the same materials but each box is different, and was very obviously intelligently designed and constructed to fulfil the intended purposes of its maker. It is *far less ridiculous* to think that the box of cereal on my refrigerator came into existence all by itself from the box in my garage; than it is to think that everything in physical existence spontaneously came into existence on its own. Do not listen to that ridiculous stupidity.

Every single bit of organic matter is purposefully functioning. It is not at all possible that this existence is spontaneously purposeless and pointless. We are each spirits living inside of complex physical machines which God individually designed to translate spiritual suggestions (Holy or demonic) into desired physical actions as per the will of its spiritual host; you (See Chapter 1; "*Attentional Awareness*"). God created all kinds of different life forms, and He *designed* specific arrangements for the nucleotides for each member of *each* species. He "wrote" *each* organic reality into existence. Genetic arrangements ("nucleotypic words") within each species' DNA produce specific physical characteristics such as hair color, height and weight potentials, skin color, teeth arrangements, kneecap shapes, metabolisms, and everything else physical.

I've written various short stories, plays, poems, and both fiction and non-fiction literature. I intentionally placed every letter, punctuation mark, word, and sentence exactly where I wanted them in each of my writings so the overall meanings of the writings would express what I intended for them to express. How are my different writings related to each other? If I used the same pen to write some of the same words to describe some similar situations in each of the writings, the words will not change themselves to be anything different from what I originally intended for them to be. My writings are letters grouped together (just like nucleotides) to make up words I've *intentionally arranged* to express my intended meanings. Jesus Christ IS God's Word (John, Chapter 1 KJV).

God wrote individual "words" (DNA) which express each form of life in existence and because He decided to use the same letters to produce different species, in no way means that the "letters" have changed themselves into different "sentences". The very idea of a ***theoretical*** evolution of life is a demonic lie. Evolution is being taught today in American schools as if it is a proven scientific fact, while there is not a shred of scientific evidence (and never will be) to validate that demonic belief. The entire idea is a lie. Evolutionary scientists emphasize that there is a three percent genetic difference between human beings and chimpanzees, but do not be confused ladies and gentlemen. More than half of our DNA is the same as a banana as well, so did we also evolve from bananas? The "three percent genetic difference" in the genes in the DNA strands between human beings and chimpanzees ***literally represents millions*** of obvious external and internal differences between the two organisms. An ignorant idiot can look at a chimpanzee and a human being and see very clear differences.

Evolutionary scientists are being used by the devil to skew study results in ways which make science seem to verify the theory of evolution. It of course, does not in any genre. Every jot and tittle of biological research not only shows that God created each organism to be whatever it is, but also that each organism has always reproduced whatever it is. If that was not true, you would not be here reading this.

Most genes are not what we call "functional genes", even though the nucleotides within each gene (Adenine (A), Cytosine (C), Guanine (G), and Thiamine (T)) are indeed "functioning" in the DNA strands composing each gene. Every bit of genetic material is doing *something* to help develop and support its manifested organism. Functional genes are genes which basically control the timing of what other genes express during physical manifestations of organic existences. Functional genes only make up a tiny percentage of the entire genetic pool of any individual organism during development, and each *functional* gene can be compared to a proverbial needle in a haystack about the size of a large city; and in some cases, a large state. Where does the instructional information and timing for functional genes come from? Who has written the genetic codes ("sentences" expressing meanings) for each living organism in existence? There are untold numbers of "piles of toothpicks" across the genetic spectrum in each organism, and each of the functional toothpicks in each pile of toothpicks is orchestrating all kinds of genetic developments in order to make each physical life form. God knew how to make trillions of organisms different from each other in this way because God knows EVERYTHING! Absolute brilliance…..

If I compare nucleotides between two different life forms (an almost innumerable amount) and then say to you, "There is only a three percent genetic difference between this species and that species"; that may be true, but I could never use that percentage in any valid way to try and support any idea which says the genetics (nucleotides) have anything to do with each other. Three percent (3%) of an almost innumerable number represents vast differences…lots and lots of differences. These differences can be very clearly seen, heard, felt, smelled and yes, even tasted between different species; say for example, between human beings and chimpanzees. The functional genes are completely different and are directing the manifestations of completely different organisms as per the will of Almighty God.

The Earth is teeming with all kinds of different life forms (we are still discovering them) and some of them are similar in many ways, but they do not interbreed nor reproduce with each other. The "missing links" in the ridiculous theory of evolution are still missing and they always will be. Do not listen to the lies and deceptions being taught today regarding evolution.

People need to stop believing they are purposeless, evolutionary, left over stardust! What difference would anyone's behavior make if we are pointless? Since people are believing more and more that they are just pointless evolutionary things, then we are experiencing previously unimaginable behaviors. People now go into public schools and into churches for instance, killing children and other innocent people for no reason. They are doing things like this because they believe the evolutionary lies that there are no ultimate consequences for anything because they are just left-over stardust. Why wouldn't everyone just do whatever they wanted to do whenever they felt like it since we only spontaneously evolved for no reason? What difference would "good and evil" make if there is no God? Well, our behaviors DO matter because GOD CERTAINLY IS. There are ALWAYS good or evil consequences to every single action or behavior we decide to exhibit, and we all know this, but we do not all acknowledge this.

If I wrote two 11,000-page books but made 300 pages of one of the books completely different from the other book including the cover and title, then the manifested differences between the books would be blatantly obvious. That is a lot of different information. Those 300 pages of different words (especially in particular places) would cause there to be extreme differences between the books. Remember the difference "did" and "died" made in the earlier example, and that was just one letter. Those books may look similar, but the differences would be plainly manifested just as they are between human beings and chimpanzees, pigs, goats, bananas, dogs, and any other organic existence with which we have genetic similarities. Human DNA is human DNA. Pig DNA is pig DNA. Chimpanzee DNA is chimpanzee DNA. Dog DNA is dog DNA and so on and so forth all across the organic spectrum. Please do not fall for these modern demonic lies. God is.

Remember that the earlier Martin "did" and Martin "died" example was only one letter's worth of difference, so imagine the possible differences with 300 entire pages worth of different letters (words/nucleotides). We did not evolve from Chimpanzees nor anything else. Sometimes characteristic differences between different species are visually obvious, and sometimes they are less physically obvious. That's just the way God made things to be, but the manifested differences between individual human beings, as well as the differences between human beings and any other kind of life form are blatantly obvious. Human beings have God-given dominion over ALL other life forms and we maintain zoos, aquariums, flocks, herds, aviaries, etc. We also keep, feed, and house dogs and other creatures as pets, while not a single other animal in existence maintains human beings as pets. We have spiritual and physical dominion over **everything** in physical existence because God created it all **for us.**

There are literally **trillions** of nucleotides in the organic DNA chains of each organism, and *each* nucleotide helps to either *manifest or influence* different physical characteristics as directed by "functional" genes to make each and every part of each organism. The genetic information in each molecule of every organism is undeniably designed and was purposefully intended. There is literally no excuse for denying God, Who is The Almighty Creator Father Who is Blessed Forever And Ever! God created everything just like He said He did, and either people can believe God in the same way young children believe and trust in their parents, or people can decide to believe the lying, eternally damned devil and then follow him into eternal damnation.

There can be between 7-8 billion human beings alive at any given moment on this planet, yet not one of them is 100% spiritually, nor physically identical to another one. God is just …. Wow! Each human being was independently created by God for **His** purposes and He gave each one of us a free spiritual will so we can do and believe as we please while still being cognizant of good and evil. "WHY" God decided, or ever decides to do **anything** is none of our business the same way it is none of my dog's business as to why I decided to put a new catalytic converter in my car, or *why* I decided to pay my neighbor's electric bill, or *why* I decided to cut my grass before my appointment. We could not understand "why" God has done anything *even if He were* to tell us. Those things are "far above our pay grade".

There was NO SPONTANEOUS beginning, and we did NOT EVOLVE from anything. The Truth NEVER changes because someone decides they don't believe it, so please do not *choose* to be a non-believer. The negative consequences of eternal damnation are far too costly. The Infinite, Eternal God Who IS Love, only asks that we believe He came here in a finite human body (Jesus), and that He killed everything negative when He took on ALL sin and negativity, then gave His physical life for each one of us. Jesus Christ then resurrected from the dead in purity, thereby giving us *all* a way to overcome *anything* negative in Jesus' Name. Sin is dead in The Name of Jesus Christ, and He is soon to return for those of us who believe Him in spirit and in truth. Jesus Christ in the flesh was certainly <u>*not*</u> that little hippie-looking dude with long brown or blonde hair in those demonic pictures we see all over the world. Those pictures "of Jesus" sitting at The Last Supper and other like depictions have been circulated worldwide and each one of those pictures is a filthy demonic lie. All of those graven images and idolized fabrications are demonic lies which are ONLY intended to equate one's particular race with Godliness. If you want to know what Jesus Christ truly looked like, read Isaiah Chapter 53. He was not physically attractive. Why would Jesus Christ have been a good-looking man going all over the place performing miracles, and healing folks? He would have been the biggest "rock star" ever for all the wrong reasons and there is no question about that. The Word of God (Jesus) is the very antithesis of physicality, so that certainly would not have made any sense at all for Jesus to have been that guy on those "church fans". That would have been a blasphemous contradiction, and God forbid!

Think about how difficult it must have been to physically look into the eyes of Jesus Christ; Who is God.... in the flesh. "...and we hid as it were, our faces from Him;..." (Isaiah

Chapter 53). Jesus Christ was not physically attractive at all and that makes perfect sense based on The Word of God. "The flesh" is the antithesis (the opposite) of the pure and righteous Word of God, and Jesus Christ IS literally the Spiritual Word of God (John, Chapter 1; KJV). Jesus Christ was literally God in "the flesh" while He walked this Earth, and "anything physical" is representational of the opposite (opposing) side of His very existence and purpose. The Bible says that Jesus Christ was physically despised and rejected, a man of sorrow and acquainted with grief. Jesus was wounded for our transgressions and bruised for our iniquities. A physical man made up of all men with white, wooly hair and bronze-looking feet/skin. Jesus Christ was as **physically** unattractive as a human being has ever been because He IS literally The Spiritual Word of God "....and we hid as it were, our faces from him..." (Isaiah 53). Jesus Christ became all of the physical burdens of mankind (**everything** negatively imaginable), then KILLED all of that when He gave His physical life while suffering the ultimate torment of torments. Believers can overcome **everything and anything** in The Name of Jesus Christ because it is already done.

Jesus got back up from the dead just like He said He would three days later leaving ALL sin and unrighteousness dead. Sin and evil have no more control over us, but ONLY through Jesus Christ is that possible. Jesus Christ is "...the way, and the truth, and the life. No man cometh unto the Father, but by Me....." (John 14:6 KJV) is what Jesus Christ said. Jesus Christ is The Only One Who could have done what He did. He is The Sacrificial Lamb of God; Hallelujah!! It is easy for people to slap, kick, curse, spit on, blaspheme, and otherwise ultimately disrespect and kill someone who is physically unattractive. In fact, the more unattractive people are physically perceived to be, then the easier it is for people to abuse, or sanction them being abused by others without interference. Jesus was every physical sorrow in existence, and was acquainted with every grief imaginable. He could not have been physically attractive.

The Eternal WORD of God is more important than anything else in physical existence because it is The One Righteously Undeniable Truth. *The Eternally Beautiful Jesus Christ* gave up ALL of that to become the physical manifestation of everything evil and ungodly so He could inherit and kill it all, thereby providing us a path to salvation. Now THAT; is ultimate Love, especially because it was also done for those who hate God.

Understanding The Truth about anything begins and ends with submitting to God; The Creator. Jesus paid the ultimate physical price for *all* of humanity so that we could be "saved" from the negative judgements which are yet to come to the world. People's continuing and worsening blasphemies against God, The Holy Spirit, and Jesus Christ are causing "the buds on the trees" to grow even more quickly, and "summertime" is very soon to come (Matthew 24: 32-33 KJV).

Again, ANY racial depictions of God, Jesus Christ, or The Holy Spirit are simply rooted in people's desires to equate their races with Ultimate Superiority, and this is the reason God told us to refrain from graven images in His second commandment. No physical image could EVER represent Almighty God, and any attempt to do so is blasphemy. God is Vastly More than we can ever imagine because God is infinite. We are finite. How could a sculptor possibly make a statue, or an artist possibly paint a picture of God? That cannot EVER be done.

Human beings are spirits which were created in the image and likeness of Almighty God, and we are residing in physical bodies made from this defiled Earth. In the next chapter, "(Chapter Three), *THE PHYSICALITY OF REPROBATE PERCEPTIONS*", I will discuss some interesting details about how and why human beings think and act as we do.

(Chapter Three)
The Physicality Of Reprobate Perceptions

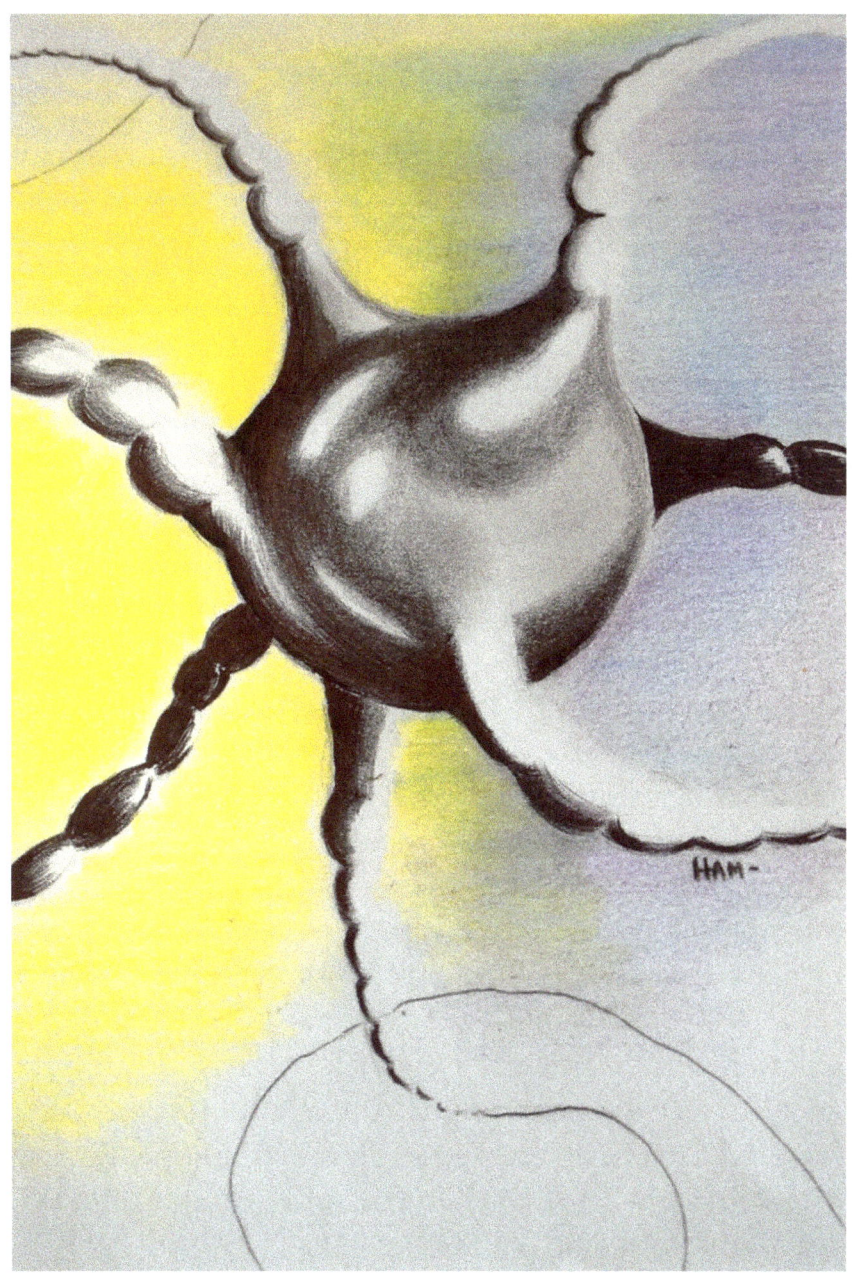

Our current perceptions have developed from consequences we have either personally experienced or that we have seen others go through; good or bad. They are self-interpreted "morals of stories" (consequential understandings). These self-interpreted morals from behavioral consequences make it difficult for each of us to perceive good and evil in our own thoughts and behaviors because all of us self-justify everything we choose to do. This is even more difficult after we have chosen to continuously repeat the same thoughts and behaviors over extended periods of time. Any behaviors we express are physical manifestations of spiritual suggestions (good or evil) we have decided to listen to, and those chosen behaviors take place after having been physically filtered through already existing (brain neuron connected/hard-wired) consequential understandings.

Our physical bodies eventually adjust to manifesting commonly used spiritual desires by solidifying/reinforcing existing neuron connections in our brains. Dendrites from neurons in our brains extend out like tree roots and are in continuous contact with other neurons which are also storing consequential information from prior behavioral decisions. Already existing dendritic contacts continuously strengthen while they also make new synaptic associations relative to our contemporary behavioral choices. This helps to make it progressively harder for us to change our behaviors. Whether or not we perceive particular behaviors as being "good" or "evil" becomes less and less important to us the more we repeat these same behaviors, especially when those behaviors are physically pleasurable to us. This is one of the reasons it is critical for each of us to spiritually check our core thoughts and behaviors for righteousness, and we are personally responsible for doing just that.

Remember, each adult is an individual spirit living inside a complex physical body over which they have complete control (if that body is healthy). Our bodies continuously convert righteous or demonic spiritual suggestions into whatever intentional behaviors we spiritually choose to physically manifest, and each person's *physical body* has pre-dispositional vulnerabilities (parameters if you will) due to its genetic makeup. The genetic makeup of each person results from the physical combinations of genetic information from the male and female genes which produced their body. Genetic parameters are physical limitations, and physical limitations *influence* (they do not dictate) the behavioral choices and decisions our residing spirits make. For example, if I am naturally physically weaker than most other boys while growing up, then I'm probably not going to grow up trying to be a neighborhood bully.

If a fella named Edwin KNOWS that his granddaddy died at a young age due to cirrhosis of the liver caused by alcoholism, and that his dad also died young from alcoholism, and that his mother is currently hospitalized because she is an alcoholic with cirrhosis of the liver, then Edwin's decisions concerning how much alcohol he drinks will certainly be influenced one way or another because he knows that most likely, alcohol will probably quickly negatively affect his liver as well if he chooses to drink. Edwin can STILL choose to do whatever he wants to do concerning alcohol though, and he can drink alcohol every single day of his adult life if he chooses to do so. He can also use his free will to decide not to drink alcohol at all under any circumstance because he knows the probable consequences.

Physical biology does not determine human behavior, but it definitely influences it. The spiritual decisions we each make

63

as independent thinkers are expressed through physical, genetically pre-dispositioned, environmentally developed, human bodies. We remember *consequences* of behavioral choices and we subconsciously store those consequential memories in either long or short-term memories depending on their relevance to our physical survival and our personal sentimental priorities. Memories of actual behaviors are not as influential on future behaviors as the *consequential memories* which resulted from those behaviors.

The way each of us act around other people is mostly a culmination of consequential memories from spiritually influenced behavioral actions we have previously undertaken while we were around other people. We spiritually analyze the consequences of our previous behaviors, and this is motivated by our personal desires. We each have a free will and whether we consider our expressed behaviors to be "good" or "evil" influences everyone differently. Some people do not seem to care about righteousness at all, but every single one of us will after our bodies are dead.

If a married man secretly begins to have a sexual relationship with his best friend's wife, then he will **initially** feel very guilty relating to what he has done. "How" he processes and deals with that guilt is up to him, but he inherently knows that is not righteous behavior. Where do human feelings of guilt before, during, and after we do evil things come from? Human beings have natural feelings of guilt relating to unrighteous behaviors whether we attempt to repress those feelings or not, and just the FACT that those feelings of guilt **naturally coexist** with negative human behaviors means that we are each unquestionably spiritually aware of "good" and "evil" (Genesis, Chapter 3 KJV). People are universally considered to be "sociopaths" when they no longer care about whether their behaviors are "good" or "evil" and these people are in fact, "reprobate". I will discuss reprobation more in detail later in this chapter.

There is a difference between human beings and animals. All animals (including beloved cats and dogs) are completely oblivious to "good" and "evil". Animals are only aware of what they need to do to survive, and this especially includes them eating and being safe. When those needs are being continuously met, animals "relax" and express whatever non-stressed and "peaceful" behaviors that particular species of animal expresses. Animals are not aware of good and evil so by using food and/or safety, human beings can train animals to do **anything** and they will do it without conscience whether it is good or evil.

The fact that some animals *show obvious **emotions*** has nothing to do with them perceiving good and evil. For example, we can train animals to attack and kill human children ***and they will do it*** without any feelings of guilt. Whatever emotions the killer animals express regarding attacking and killing human children will **only** be geared towards their perceived owners'/trainers' satisfaction level with them. Whether or not they think their owners are pleased with them, or they will receive some kind of food or safety reward is all that matters to any animal after they have been trained. Animals' emotions will be either excitement because they have killed human children and satisfied their owners'/trainers' desires, or disappointment because they did not kill any children and therefore their owners/trainers will not reward them. They will not think about what they have done later on and feel guilty about having killed those children. There are no animals which naturally hunt human beings. Even when creatures such as sharks or bears attack human beings, they rarely consume them. Animals inherently understand that human beings have God-given dominion over them, and this precludes them from hunting us.

Human beings are most certainly aware of good and evil. The adulterous man in the earlier example in this chapter ended up having sex with his best friend's wife because he initially listened to a negative spiritual influence (a demon), and she did too. After his first sexual encounter with her, he most likely had his strongest feelings of guilt as one of his consequential memories, and the things he will mostly remember about being sexual with her depends a great deal on the amount of physical pleasure (or lack thereof) he experienced with her. Guilty feelings from doing something wrong become **progressively less associated** with consequential memories if "the wrong" we have done produced positive or pleasurable feelings. The opposite is true as well. Guilty feelings become **more associated** with consequential memories (we feel more guilty) when behaviors produce negative feelings. This is not as strong, nor as obvious with sociopathic or otherwise insensitive (reprobate) people.

"Adultery man's" future behaviors towards his best friend's wife will depend on which spiritual influences he contemporarily chooses to listen to (either Holy or evil), but his behaviors will be heavily influenced by the already existing consequential memories from his previous sexual encounters with her. Perhaps the affair was problematic, stressful, and negative for him because not only did they get caught by her husband, but he also contracted a sexually transmitted disease from the married woman. She is also now pregnant with what may be his child.

Those are extremely negative consequences, and his feelings of guilt will be stronger and last longer than they otherwise would have. If he had pleasurable sexual experiences with her; they did not get caught by his friend or his own wife, he did not contract any venereal diseases, and she is not pregnant at all; then any feelings of guilt he had will probably not be as strong, nor last as long. Whatever the results turn out to be, the *consequences* of what happened will undoubtedly affect his behavior towards her and other married women from then on. Again, *consequential memories* from behaviors influence future behaviors far more than memories of actual behaviors. Of course, the man in this adultery example will remember some of the actual physical positions and feelings which occurred during their sexual interludes, but what happened **as a result** of those experiences will more heavily influence his future decisions in similar situations.

Our personal long and short-term goals and desires, as well as our individual determinations to do what we want to do all strongly influence how we utilize consequential memories. We spiritually classify the consequences of our past behaviors according to self-perceived, self-preservational needs, and that information is then prioritized as much as possible by each of us in different situations. Repetitious usage of the same consequential information in different situations eventually becomes recognizable to others as behavioral consistencies, and behavioral consistencies are personality indicators about the person (spirit) inside that body.

The more we choose to manifest behaviors, the more the physical neurons in each of our brains relate previously unassociated consequential memories with newly related consequential memories regarding those behaviors. When

67

we physically manifest the same spiritual thoughts and behaviors in similar situations, then the physical neurons associated with those thoughts and physical behaviors become more and more securely connected to each other and soon become capable of almost manifesting "default" physical behaviors. "Almost" because we each have a free will and we can consciously overcome "default behaviors" if we choose to do so. Again, repeated behavioral responses become more and more physically "hard-wired" in our brains with relative consequential information, and this makes it easier to self-justify the things we continuously decide to say and do.

If a girl named Sherri is almost always alone because she chooses to be by herself, then she is alone because she acts in certain ways and says certain things that make people leave her alone. She knows how to make people leave her alone because in her past she has used similar techniques and words that have caused people to leave her alone. She has chosen to use the same body languages, gestures, words, and other behaviors which produce her desired consequences; ultimately being left alone. Things like this come from consequential memories.

These same mental processes are at work for example, when linebackers playing American football hit opposing running backs extra hard on plays when the running backs do not even have the ball. If the consequences normally result in less than average games for those running backs, then the linebackers will continue to try and smash running backs like that because their teams gain defensive advantages. The linebackers may not remember each hit in each game, but they certainly remember the consequences of executing those hits, and using those memories makes those linebackers better players. This is a good example of how positive consequential memories combined with physical abilities to perform activities, increase a person's ability to produce outstanding results; especially in sports. When physically gifted people *spiritually* identify physical actions they can perform which help them realize their desired goals, then of course they will often use those same actions again and again. They have made those actions and moves before and they already know how defenders will respond (consequential memories) to them.

Great athletes' bodies almost instantly manifest their spiritual inputs and produce physical actions based on their past actions and their different opponents' past reactions. I call this "consequential intellect", and great athletes seem to have a higher-level of consequential intellect than most of the other athletes they compete with and against. Great athletes also inherently understand the laws of physics as they relate to angles, movements, and velocities.

Absolutely great athletes such as Michael Jordan, Tom Brady, Cynthia Cooper, Muhammed Ali, Larry Bird, Deion Sanders, LeBron James, Florence Griffith Joyner, Tiger Woods, Jerry Rice, Candace Parker, Hank Aaron, Jim Brown, Jackie Robinson, Sue Bird, Barry Sanders, Edson Arantes do Nascimento (Pele'), Caitlin Clark, Albert Pujols, and the absolute litany of other fantastically gifted athletes like Jackie Joyner Kersey, Diana Taurasi, Walter Payton, *and a host of others* from all over this world, clearly display a higher level of "consequential intellect". They understand physical actions and reactions more quickly than others around them because they are utilizing deeper levels of consequential memories. They are quickly thinking things such as, "If I move like this or if I move like that, then this or that will happen as a result.", or "If I quickly look that way then ease over in my lane, such and such will happen…..", and so on and so forth. These are examples of spiritual inputs which are almost instantly physically manifested by great athletes while they are in the process of playing a sport. They have quick consequential understandings. Elite athletes indeed operate consequentially and are physically gifted enough to almost instantly physically manifest their spiritual desires. This is why they always seem to be "a step or two ahead" of their competitors. The athletes I mentioned are only SOME of the elite athletes from all kinds of different sports who demonstrate higher levels of consequential intellect; there are many more. Consequential thinking is how we each perceive the world.

Our "perceptions" can be "physically rewired" (so to speak) in our brains because our perceptions are *physically* represented in our brains via physical synapse connections between neurons; neurons which store memories of consequences. Is it "right" or "wrong" for a black man who was born and raised in a segregated southern American town to think that *all* white people are mean and violent if all the white people he has experienced in his lifetime have been mean and violent towards him and other black people? If this man maintains negative thoughts about all white people, are his negative thoughts about all white people justified? With each incident of racial hatred he either hears about or personally experiences, his consequential perceptions from those memories stimulate and further strengthen the physical synaptic connections already established in his brain between neurons which store negative consequential memories regarding white people. Stereotypical thoughts are not always formed by choice, nor are they necessarily correctly spiritually self-perceived as being "good" or "evil".

Some people do not believe that human beings have a free will and they claim that this existence is predestined. They say we do not have a choice in how anything turns out in the end because God already knows everything about everything. That is one of the most ridiculous things I've personally ever heard because it is an indisputable FACT that we CAN each do or say anything we want to do or say at any given moment including right now, at this very second. Whenever we want to do or say anything we can imagine to anyone else at any time, we absolutely CAN. This is what it means to have a free will. We can do whatever we want to do. You or I can get up right now and say something offensive to someone nearby and then slap them in the face for no reason at all. We each; however, know that there are definite consequences to every action we decide to take, so we can just as easily get up and pat someone on the back and tell them how much we love and appreciate them. Most people control themselves and do not say or do offensive things to others without provocation because there are always consequences to everything we do. We each indeed have a free will and we continuously manifest whatever behaviors we choose to display. God knows everything that can be known; past, present, and future. God gave each of us a free will, and He already knows how every single one of us is going to use it. Choose wisely.

As we each mature from children into adults, we become more and more spiritually responsible for evaluating ourselves for righteousness in every aspect of our lives. We must each spiritually examine our existing thought patterns, stereotypes, and general "default" behaviors when it comes to righteousness. Our spiritually/behaviorally intended words and actions are *filtered* through our physical brains at manifestation, and when people's physical brains are full of negatively wired consequential information about situations, people, circumstances, etc., then spiritually intended words and behaviors sometimes physically manifest differently than they were spiritually intended. Negative things either get blurted out, or negative actions and abuses occur.

People can spiritually KNOW they are wrong about physically harboring negative ideas about other kinds of people, yet they still **allow** those physically negatively wired beliefs to influence their negative physical actions against other kinds of people. We often hear people say things like, "I didn't mean for that to come out like that.", or "I didn't mean to say it like that, but you know what I mean….", or "Oops, did I say that out loud?".

We feel guilty or conflicted about some of our moods, words, or behaviors, yet we still say or do those same things again anyway. If physically formed consequential thoughts (brain neuron synaptic connections) and memory associations are not spiritually *self-investigated* for righteousness and then willfully rewired by The Holy Spirit, then negative brain synapse connections will continue to strengthen while at the same time making new connections which help us self-justify our behavioral thoughts and actions. The longer we exist without salvation in The Name of Jesus Christ, it becomes more and more difficult for us to change our negative thoughts and expressed behaviors. People develop negative mindsets such as, "That's just the way those people are!", or "I've always known that about those people anyway!", while trying to justify saying or doing negative things against them because they "know what they are talking about.". People go so far as to attempt to justify murdering men, women, and children because of their different races, religious beliefs, lifestyles, etc. Again, in **their** minds *they know what they are talking about and they know what they are doing.*

The soul and the mind are different. The "mind" is an individual soul's "intent" in its purest form. The mind is a person's deepest spiritual intent to express whatever they choose to express. It is an intent because it is "my" mind, and "I" possess it. Who is the "I" which has that intent... who possesses that mindset? It is me, my soul. The soul is where our spirits are combined with our physical bodies (Genesis 2:7). Our "minds" can be "set" because physical neurons in our brains start interconnecting more and more with consequential memories if we repeat the same thoughts or behaviors too many times.

God will eventually give us over to a reprobate **mind** if we decide to keep manifesting a negative behavior again and again (Romans 1:28-32 KJV). That means a person will not receive any more righteous spiritual suggestions regarding a particular behavior, and without righteous suggestions from The Holy Spirit, it is very difficult to manifest/express any behaviors which go against our already existing "mindsets" (the "consequential hardwiring/physical neurons in our brains).

A person who is reprobate in a particular sin has almost completely lost their physical ability to control that sin. The physical connections in their brains almost "automatically" manifest negative comments or behaviors because that person has chosen to use those comments or behaviors too many times before in too many different situations. Even though their spirits may recognize that they shouldn't be saying or doing whatever it is they are saying or doing, that person is far less able to control their physical responses to certain triggers. People, situations, places and circumstances may each act as triggers for those reprobate behaviors. People with reprobate minds are; however, still cognizant of good and evil and we are each always responsible for our actions.

Being reprobate concerning a behavior leads to people having trouble recognizing how their behaviors and actions are being perceived by other people. Reprobate people do not care about how they are being perceived. For example, a reprobate person who is strung out on illegal drugs (because at earlier times in their lives *they decided* they would not stop using drugs despite numerous warnings and opportunities to stop) shows little concern for how they are acting around other people in their immediate area, even though they may be standing on top of different cars at 3a.m. loudly singing Christmas carols …. in July. Their spirits recognize that they are behaving abnormally because they already know it is not normal for anyone to be standing on cars behaving like they are currently behaving; yet they are still doing it. They also know they haven't done that in the past, nor have they seen anyone else do it. They know that…but they are doing it anyway.

When people do abnormal things in public, then they are immediately perceived by other "normal" people as being potentially dangerous because they are acting outside the bounds of "normal" public behavior. As we spiritually exist in these physical bodies, we are each fully aware of how we are being spiritually perceived by others and how to conduct ourselves accordingly. When people either do not care about, or are not aware of how they are being perceived socially, then this increases the potential for problems to arise. Parents and other responsible adults in societies worldwide try to teach children culturally relevant behavioral norms and parameters, and each "normal" human being in every civil society is consistently aware of how they are being perceived by people. How we behave, how we construct our sentences, how we walk, smell, talk, dress, etc., is critically important because none of us "normal people" want to be perceived by others as being dangerous, stupid, smelly, psychotic, or otherwise abnormal. This has been, is, and will be true in any culture.

Negative spirits (demons) attack people with evil suggestions when people are reprobate. Reprobate people only have their self-will with which to defend themselves against negative hardwiring in the brain. They can always use their will (personal spiritual determination) to express righteous behaviors which go against the influences of hard-wired behaviors. A person's desire to express righteous behaviors while they are reprobate has got to be strong at that point in order for that person to overcome their negative verbal and behavioral "default" expressions. They are operating from a reprobate condition, but they still have a free will and can always turn to God in The Name of Jesus Christ.

Committing a sin and *being reprobate* in that sin are two different things. This reality is true for **any** unrighteous behavior. For example, if a heterosexual man has a sexual experience with another man, then he is not automatically "gay", nor is he reprobate concerning that behavior. That man has indeed engaged in homosexual behaviors, but since he has not continued that behavior to the point of reprobation, then he is not "gay". He will not be professing homosexuality to anyone because he is not reprobate concerning homosexuality. Only a person who is reprobate concerning homosexuality can profess themselves to be "gay". There are many convicted murderers in prisons all over the world right now who will openly profess to anyone that they will kill someone again if they are released. These folks are reprobate concerning killing, and they are proud to be murderers. A person who has murdered someone before and is truly remorseful about having committed the murder is not reprobate concerning killing. Just because a person has told lies before (and we all have), then he/she is not reprobate concerning lying. You are not a habitual liar. If someone **chooses** to lie all the time about practically anything for no reason, then they are almost certainly reprobate concerning lying. They know they lie a lot, and they know that everyone else knows that they lie a lot, yet they continue lying and do not care what other people think about it. They are reprobate concerning lying. If someone has stolen something before, that does not make them reprobate concerning stealing. A kleptomaniac is a habitual thief who is reprobate concerning stealing and they take pride in stealing. All of these demonstrate the difference between sinning, and being reprobate in a sin.

We each began to spiritually experience our physical existences the instant our sperm fertilized our egg. Temperamentally, we are already who we are at birth and this is why babies are behaviorally different from each other. We are individual spirits born into this physical world in small, uncoordinated, "unprogrammed machines" (human bodies). Up to this exact point in time, we have each perceived the world in our own ways *through* each of our own bodies as we have each experienced different situations and circumstances at different stages during our lives. We have spiritually become more and more aware of our physical bodies the more they have developed, and we are continually improving our abilities to communicate in different ways so that we can share our perceptions of this physical life with each other.

Human beings are unlike anything else in physical existence, and we express ourselves through our individual, ever-changing bodies. We are each (almost) fully actualized spirits born into a physical "machine" (a body), and our bodies are environmentally influenced. Our bodies eventually develop into a physical organism which we completely spiritually control, but we cannot be fully spiritually actualized until we accept Jesus Christ as our Lord and Savior by The Holy Spirit of God. God IS eternity and He is the afterlife people always speak of.

We will ALL answer to God in the end. Once our physical bodies develop enough for us to express our exact spiritual desires (post-adolescence), then we each become 100% accountable to God for what we direct our bodies to do. From that point forward, we strive to become independently physically actualized. We are born spiritually actualized enough to become adults in this physical realm, but only after salvation in The Name of Jesus Christ by The Holy Spirit can a person be fully *spiritually* actualized. This is what it means to be "born again". We will each either enjoy or suffer the consequences of how we have directed our bodies to operate in this physical realm when we spiritually stand before God after our bodies have died. Again, our bodies are directly comparable to the personal automobiles we drive. Automobiles will **only** do what we direct them to do while we are in them, and we as the "drivers" are 100% responsible for what our vehicles do. If they (bodies or vehicles) malfunction because we did not take care of them, then that is our fault as well.

We each need to investigate ourselves when it comes to maintaining negatively formed thoughts and behaviors towards other people, even if they seem to be justified. Some people decide not to change at all and go through their lives full of hatred and confusion directed towards other people. The black man in the earlier example who grew up in the segregated south, is still **not** justified if he goes through the rest of his life hating and negatively stereotyping *all* white people because of his personal experiences. Although it is certainly understandable for him to have developed negative consequential memories which may manifest as negative thoughts and behaviors towards the entire Caucasian race, he is still spiritually responsible as an adult to examine his own thoughts and behaviors for righteousness so as ***not*** to errantly generalize his negative stereotypical thinking to *all* white people. The sooner he does this, the less likely he is to become reprobate concerning whatever negativities he may be harboring. The white people who *caused* his negative perceptions to occur in the first place were most likely already reprobate concerning hating black people. They had already become almost completely limited to physically translating negative spiritual influences into negative behaviors against black people because of their mindsets.

We are ALL born into this sinful physical realm, and we ALL need to be "mentally rewired" in order to attain righteous thinking. *Righteous rewiring* occurs **only** through salvation in the Name of Jesus Christ by the renewing of our minds by the Holy Spirit of God (Romans 12:2; Ephesians 4:23; KJV). Our behaviors are conscious decisions we continuously make, and reprobate or not we will each ultimately be held accountable for them.

Can we scientifically study the spiritual realm as it relates to human beings? Can we scientifically study spiritual interactions in this physical realm? Science pertaining to the spirit realm is extremely difficult (if not impossible) to perform and in the next chapter, "Chapter 4; *MODERN SCIENCE: SPIRIT REALM RESEARCH*", I will discuss some of the reasons this is true.

(CHAPTER FOUR)
MODERN SCIENCE: SPIRITUAL/
PHYSICAL REALM RESEARCH

We can only *scientifically* research matter in this physical realm; not the spiritual realm. Scientifically researching the spirit realm for interactions in human circumstances can cause all kinds of confusion because it is very difficult (if not impossible) to reliably do so. Each human being is a vastly different combination of spiritual and physical variables, so to perform valid experiments which consistently show spiritual interactions in human circumstances, it is imperative that the human subjects participating in these kinds of studies be separated into specific groups first. The initial test subject selection standards need to be entirely different from normal scientific test-subject selection standards because the test subjects (people) will always each be at different levels of "operational" spiritual beliefs and faiths. Some people are religious and strictly follow all kinds of different customs and traditions, while some other people are believers in Jesus Christ by The Holy Spirit, and yet some others claim to be atheists. There are also those who "claim" to believe in Jesus Christ, but do not. There are all kinds of other people who believe whatever else they spiritually believe, and spiritual study results will be different for each of those groups of people. Before performing any valid spiritual research, these absolutely critical distinctions must be made, and herein lies the major problem.

Accurately comprehending spiritual distinctions between test subjects will directly determine the validity of the research results. A "***religious***" person for example, may go to church every Sunday and may adhere to most of the customs and traditions of that particular denomination of "church people", but that person may not have true *faith* that God can make physical differences in their life. "Religious" people follow customs, traditions, and behaviors which are relevant to whichever denomination they belong, and they may religiously worship the devil or anything else for that matter. Some religious people only believe *some parts* of The Holy Bible, while in comparison, a **saved, born-again "believer"** is a person who **knows** that the complete Word of God is all they need for everything in the Name of Jesus Christ by The Holy Spirit in **any** situation ever. There is a night and day difference between those two groups.

The problem with scientifically testing for spiritual interactions in human circumstances is, "How can the aforementioned test-subject selection standards be determined without conflictions before each spiritual experiment to ensure each experiment's validity?" The answer is that those distinctions **cannot** be made reliably enough for valid spiritual experimentation because human beings are not capable of physically making those spiritual judgements. We *could* secretly study how potential test subjects handle pre-arranged challenging situations and then based on those observations, separate them into particular groups, but even that will not work. We will never be able to classify with *scientific* certainty, another person's spiritual relationship with God. We would be attempting to sit in the **unattainable** seat of judgement if we took that approach.

Another problem with making these distinctions is that a person's behavior (religious or otherwise) is not necessarily indicative of what that person spiritually believes. "**Religion**" refers to *specific physical behaviors and activities seemingly carried out for spiritual purposes, be they righteous or demonic.* Church customs, denominational traditions, and other such variables are all facets of religion, and individuals can indeed be strictly "religious". "**Belief**" on the other hand, refers to *an* *individual's* **certainty** *about the* **reality** *of God in The Name of Jesus Christ, by The Holy Spirit.*

A person's behaviors and activities can *sometimes* be indicators of their levels of "belief", but that is a very unreliable way to try and determine someone's independent spiritual acknowledgement of God. Faith in God in The Name of Jesus Christ *can indeed* change physical situations and circumstances, but the problem of being able to **reliably** separate *religious people, believers, agnostics, and atheists* within study groups for scientific experimentation has got to be resolved in order to show this and again, that is humanly impossible. Even if we **could** somehow make reliable, accurate, and valid spiritual test subject determinations for scientific purposes, then it wouldn't matter anyway because God can never be "scientifically provable" (Mark 8:12; Luke 11:29; Matthew 16:4; KJV). God is not subject to our sign-seeking verifications of His existence whether our desires are for scientific purposes or not, and why would He **ever** be (John 20:29;KJV)?

We either walk by faith or we do not "walk" at all because it is impossible for someone to physically prove to someone else that God exists. That being said, all anyone ever has to do is stop and think about EVERYTHING going on *at the same time all over the entire world.* Think about all the coordinated, interconnected natural occurrences (clouds, rivers, lava, moss, evaporations, snowstorms, winds, etc.), and the billions of human beings cooking, eating, paying bills, having babies, hunting, playing, driving, etc., all at the same time. *God has already spiritually and physically proven Himself to every single one of us* by His creations, AND there is nothing else which could possibly have been done; "It is finished" (John 19:30 KJV). Either you believe The Holy

Word of God or you do not, and just the fact that **everything** is functioning together with many unquestionably designed purposes whether we discover those functions or not, speaks for itself. God is.

Modern science is limited to attempting to explain physical facts without the ability to understand the spiritual truths about those same facts. Scientific studies involve observing and manipulating **physical** matter to learn more about it and because we cannot likewise scientifically study the spiritual realm, then we cannot learn about spiritual realities in that same manner. The worldwide public is being lied to by the devil through modern scientists because now "the professionals" are attempting to explain everything physical as being spontaneous things which "luckily" came into existence all by themselves. Many modern scientists in various genres have the audacity to claim they can fully explain the origins of everything without any Creator having been involved via "the Standard Model". This is happening in **every** discipline of modern science because we are born into sin and shaped in iniquity and when people are not "saved" from the demonic confusion and its consequences, then their interpretations of anything will always end up being wrong. There is no way any of us can know we are being lied to about anything until we learn (or unless we already know) the truth. This is important because we are all born into an atmosphere saturated with demonic lies about everything, and we do not realize that until we hear and accept The Truth. We need to be saved from eternal damnation.

Modern humanity seems to believe that human beings have something to do with the existences of the physical variables we scientifically study. When scientists *discover* already existing physical processes, systems, forces, or any other ongoing functions in the universe, then those functions are credited to the scientists who discovered them with zero mention of God The Father, Who created them. Think about it; when someone *discovers* something, then that "something" has to have already been there before they discovered it. Each part of that something was already performing different purposes which were helping to make the entire system operate. Before we ever **discovered** "anything", God had already designed that "something" and every other "something" in existence and put it wherever it was so that it could do whatever it was doing...then we found it.

If a person has never heard of a train before and then they suddenly discover a locomotive engine with freight cars attached to it sitting on a track in the woods somewhere, then they SHOULD DEFINITELY be able to deduce that someone designed and built this complicated machine as well as the specifically designed (for the train) tracks it is sitting on. Every single part of that train engine has different purposes for existing, and each part of the train purposefully relates to every other part of the train. All the parts of the train function together for the clear purpose of safely moving the heavy train engine and all of the attached cars in a controlled manner along the tracks it is sitting on.

If the person who *discovered* the train believes that the train, the attached cars, and the tracks spontaneously appeared all by themselves wherever they were discovered, then almost everyone would consider the discoverer of the train to be an idiot...a deranged lunatic. The exact same atheistic scientists claiming that this universe appeared all by itself would have that person committed to an asylum for telling people that the train spontaneously appeared. Those same scientists would turn right around and go to work the same night and look into the night sky from powerful telescopes and say, "This happened all by itself...". Some of them would go into a biological lab somewhere the following day and study trillions of nucleotides in organic DNA strands and then look up from the electron microscope and say, "This all happened by itself...". Those things are almost infinitely more complicated than any train mankind has ever, will ever, or can ever build. Please do not allow yourselves to be mislead. We live in an atmosphere of the most foolishly demonic lies which have ever existed.

Let's pretend "Keith" is the person who discovered that train on the tracks. Keith tells the world that he believes the train created itself and then he begins to come up with some *theoretical explanations* as to how he thinks that could have happened. The scientific world then names the train "Keith's Train". Keith had nothing to do with the train already being there and already being completely functional, but now it's "Keith's Train". Keith only discovered the train already sitting on the tracks wherever it already was. Soon, Keith and others begin to conjure up ridiculous ideas and theories based on impossible concepts about how the train and the tracks could have spontaneously developed. More and more people begin to listen to Keith and the others' explanations about the train and the longer the people listen, the more they believe them because after all, Keith is the one who discovered the train, and the others are the ones who are professionally studying it. People then begin to believe that Keith and others "know what they are talking about." Modern science is on the same ridiculous path regarding God's creation (everything in existence). ".....Professing themselves to be wise, they became fools....." (Romans Chapter 1:20-32; KJV).

Modern scientists are doing this with spontaneous big bang/evolutionary theories. "Kepler's Laws" mathematically describe already existing, perfectly organized, balanced relationships between the sun and orbiting matter in our solar system. These *obviously designed* relationships have been ongoing since God created them, so how then can they be "Kepler's Laws"?! Did Johannes Kepler have anything to do with placing the planets where they are? Does Kepler have anything to do with keeping the forces making the planets rotate and orbit the sun operating? No, he doesn't (Job 38:4 KJV). "Isaac Newton's" Law of Universal Gravitation states that every particle in the universe attracts every other particle in the universe with varying degrees of force. If that is true, did Newton create that law, or did he only discover some already existing aspects about gravity and write about them? Yep…. Newton **only discovered** some already existing aspects about gravity and documented them. "Pascal's Principle" states that changes in pressure applied to an enclosed fluid is transmitted undiminished to every point of the fluid, and to the walls of its container. Why is this referred to as "Pascal's Principle"? Did Pascal create this principle? Has Pascal ever created anything?! No. He only figured out how to write formulas so the rest of us can better understand force parameters and other characteristics about contained fluids. Where was Pascal when God created force parameters? Was Pascal God's advisor? C'mon now. "Archimedes' Principle" describes how and why objects float. Objects float because God created buoyant forces (air/water ratios, displacement, etc.) and various other conditions for floatation to take place, and that is the only reason objects float. Again, Archimedes only discovered and described some of the (already purposefully designed) mathematical mechanisms of displacement and buoyancy.

These kinds of blasphemies go on and on throughout modern science, and all these modern atheists' intentional emphasis on this existence being a pointless spontaneous "thing" with no purpose is fueling that disrespect. It would be impossible for any kind of **consistencies** to exist if our existence was spontaneous. Spontaneity would be the fabric of the universe but that is impossible, and every single human being KNOWS in the deepest part of them that this is true. Purposed, functionally coordinated, operational motion is the fabric of this universe.

Nothing could be reliably consistent if everything was spontaneous because surely **everything** would spontaneously change every now and then for absolutely no reason at all. It would be impossible for any organic life form to reproduce consistently if everything was spontaneous because of the multi-millions of perfectly coordinated, complex biological processes which must take place in sequence the reproductive systems of **each** organic existence in order for reproduction to occur. If things were spontaneous, then each species would reproduce whatever happened to develop (if they reproduced at all) because of all of the biological inconsistencies "spontaneity" would certainly produce. God created this purpose-filled universe, and it is a scientific fact that there is no such thing as spontaneity. There is *no such thing as spontaneity* because we can accurately calculate probabilities, even though we do not as of yet understand all of the mechanisms causing scientifically probable outcomes. We know that they exist however, because we can indeed predict probabilities. Spontaneity offers no such thing **at any** level. There could be no such thing as predictability.

When God created the *spirit* of man, He created male AND female spirits (Gen 1:27; KJV). *After* that, He made one human body from the earth, and *then* blew the spirit of man (male and female) into that one physical body (Adam), "….and man became a living soul" (Gen 2:7 KJV). He *then* physically separated the female body (Eve) from that same Adam body (Gen 2:21-22; KJV), thereby forming two *spiritually and physically different* human beings having the same spirit of man. There are spiritual and physical men, and there are spiritual and physical women. Be very careful about claiming that God has made mistakes with human spirits and bodies because you are indeed calling God a liar. This is the same reason the devil is now eternally damned, so check yourselves because every(**body**) is going to die, and every spirit will then be held accountable (Rev 21:8 KJV), (1 Cor 6:9-13 KJV).

The **instant** a male's sperm penetrates a female's egg, the very first thing that happens is the sex of the body to be "manufactured" is physically determined. The cells HAVE to know what to begin to make so from that instant forward, a boy or a girl begins to grow inside the mother's womb. The physical processes which take place as we are being physically formed in the womb intentionally manifest God's desires for each one of our physical beings, and even though we may not understand God's purposes for "manufacturing" some bodies as He does, that is HIS business. That physical body will be the "vehicle" in which that spirit will reside during their temporary existence in this physical realm.

Each body develops with unique characteristics, and *any* of the body parts can "be manufactured" with what we sometimes perceive as "other than normal" characteristics. Some folks are born with unusually large hands or feet, and some people have big heads. Other people have abnormally long tongues or arms and in extremely rare cases, physical bodies develop with what seems to be both male and female genitalia. These bodies still either develop with a womb for reproductive purposes (eggs-female), or they do not (sperm-male). People are either men or women (Genesis 1:27, 5:2 KJV), and to declare anything else is to call God a liar. If a man is born with an unusually large penis, is he "another sex"? If a woman is born with an unusually large vagina, is she another sex? If a man or woman is born with an otherwise deformed sexual organ, are they another sex? No; they are not. There are men, and there are women inside those bodies. May God help you understand this if this is a struggle for you. It shouldn't be.

In modern society, people are intentionally making themselves appear to be whatever sex they desire, and the desire to appear androgynous and live alternative sexual lifestyles is popular in the modern worl. People can legally claim to be a man and/or a woman at any given time. Modern "understandings" about human sexuality are becoming more and more confused. People are having their physical bodies surgically manipulated, and they are also taking hormones to look like whichever sex they choose to want to look like. None of that matters because we **each spiritually know** which sex we are, and you'd better believe that God knows that as well. Whether or not we each accept and function in this life as "who we are" is between each person and God Almighty. God created each of us **to be** and **to do** whatever it is He created us to be and to do, and whether we fulfil our purposes or not is up to each one of us. The devil is the author of confusion (1 Corinthians 14:33), and it is clear that people in the world right now are very sexually confused.

Whenever someone says they are a man or a woman trapped in an opposite sex body, then they are acknowledging (albeit with a confused, demonic twist) their *spiritual* AND *physical* existences. There is indeed a tiny percentage of people who are born with sexual organs or other body parts that do not seem to physically match their spiritual male or female beings. For instance there are women with excessive body hair and/or masculine builds, and there are also men with protruded breasts and feminine-looking hips. I am certainly **not anybody's judge.** That seat is FAR too big for my little hind part, so I am in no way judging anybody; I am just telling you the truth. The fact is that these popular new modern claims as to males being trapped in female bodies and vice-versa, are mostly based on people's personal desires to make modern sexual lifestyle choices.

During fetal development, birth abnormalities can occur at **any** place on the human body, but regardless of the extent of a living person's physical challenges (physically incapacitating birth defects for example), each of us KNOW there is either a male or female human spirit inside of each of those physical bodies. All over the world, people naturally take care of and dignify other people who were born not physically capable of taking care of themselves. We hospitalize or otherwise take care of people who are born with physical disabilities because we all KNOW there is either a male or a female spirit (person) inside each one of those physically challenged bodies. The instant our physical sex is established we become living souls and again, this is the very first thing which happens at conception. We become individual male or female spirits operating inside individual physical bodies in this physical realm. There are "conjoined twins", but they each have completely different personalities and this is absolute proof.

Carbon is the only "true" organic element in existence because it is the only element existing in EVERY form of life, and no carbon has ever been detected, found, or otherwise located on any other planet, moon, asteroid, etc. Carbon is abundantly found in rocks, sand, the oceans, and elsewhere in the Earth's atmosphere (because the Earth itself is alive). All neutral (basic) Carbon – 12 atoms contain 6 protons, 6 neutrons, and 6 electrons, and it is ***not a coincidence*** that in The Holy Bible the number 666 is referred to as "the number of man" (Rev 13:18). 666 is the name of organic evil, and Revelation Chapter 13, verses 16, 17, and 18 all make this very clear. Mankind IS that organic evil, and this is why we must be saved by The Blood of Jesus Christ. Everything physical exists **for** mankind, and God gave us dominion over all of it. Because mankind turned away from God, this entire physical realm (including all life) will end when Jesus Christ comes back, and He is very soon to do so. 666 (Carbon) is in **every** life form and in most of the other physical existences here on earth as well. Why haven't we been able to find any carbon on any other planet, moon, asteroid, comet, etc., which we have investigated? Answer: Because there is none. Humanity is THE dominant life form in this universe and God created this entire universe as well as the living Earth itself to contain us. It takes an atmosphere as large as this universe to contain mankind, so please do not be fooled by all these devilish, spontaneous, evolutionary lies.

Because we are organic physical-realm existences, then we are subject to the physical effects of time, and I will discuss some interesting, thought-provoking aspects about time in the following chapter, (Chapter 5) "WHAT IS "TIME"?"

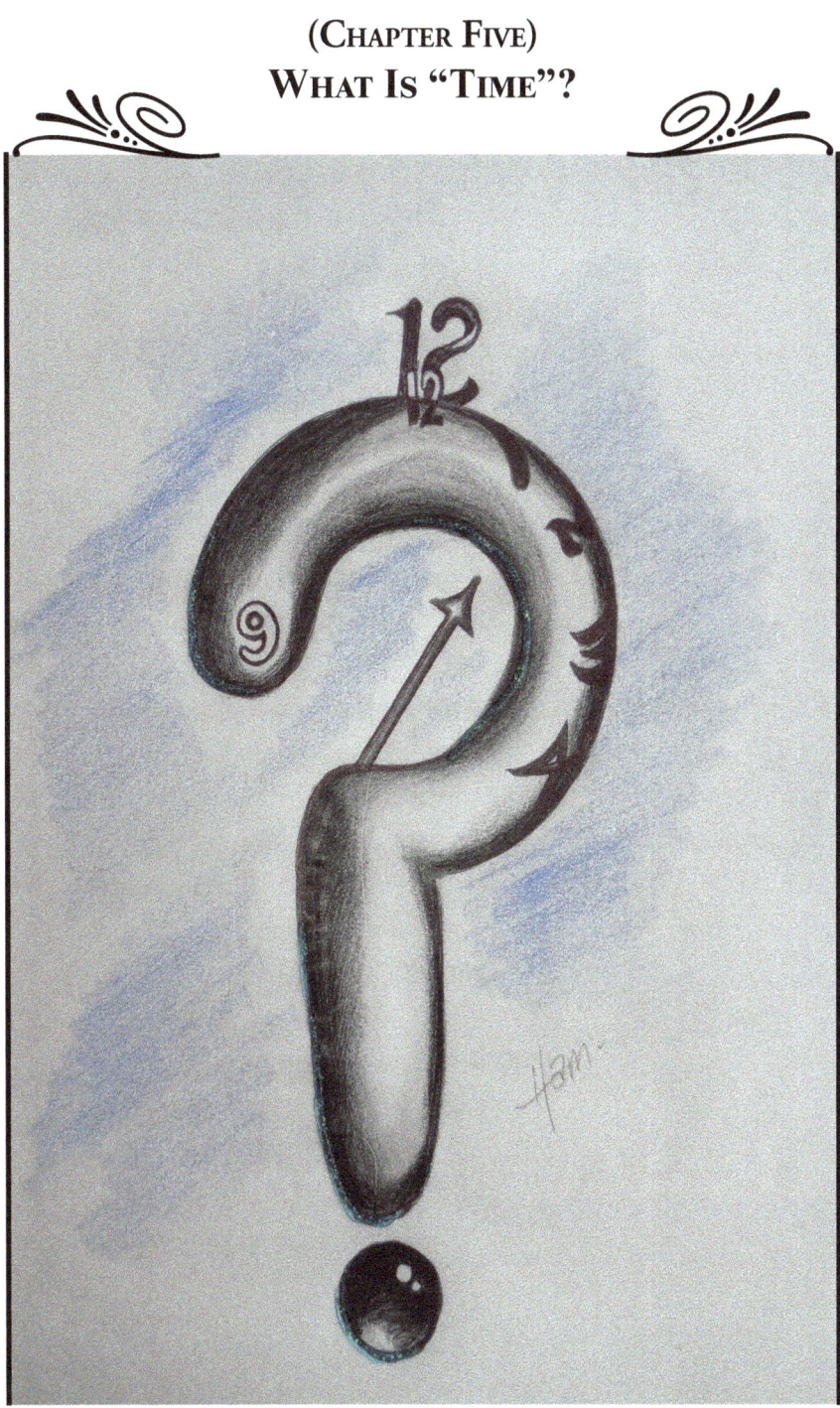

Every molecule making up physical matter in this physical realm is in motion; therefore, physical matter is literally "time", and time will definitely end (Rev 10:5-6, KJV). "Time" (**everything** that means to any of us right now) only exists in this physical realm and does not exist in the spiritual realm. Physical "time" began when God created the physical universe (Gen 1: 1, KJV) and this was *before* Adam and Eve were physically made. We have no idea how long everything else had already existed before we were created (Gen 1:26-31, KJV), so our academic notations of time such as "3 O'clock", "March 27", 1973, etc., are only arbitrary concepts derived from the initial 7 days of creation as described in the Holy Bible. Our academic notations of time have also resulted from us documenting regularly occurring natural events such as predictable positions and phases of the moon, identifiable times for sunrises and sunsets, indicators of changing seasons, etc. The longer we exist, the more details we have been able to document about regularly occurring natural events, and because modern scientists can now study physical facts and technological details, they carnally deny The Truth concerning those same events (they deny that God created everything because it doesn't seem physically possible).

We would have a much more realistic understanding of time if we would study physical matter from the truthful perspective of creation, but modern man has turned away from God. The very nature of mankind is evil, and this is why atheists go through great efforts to try and interpret "science" as if it goes against the written Word of God, when it does not. To even begin to construct a concept of a Godless "spontaneous beginning", a fabricated history of time made up of billions and trillions of years had to have been constructed. The physically impossible, spontaneous processes atheists say occurred to produce what we know as this universe, could only have been possible in a comic book after zillions of years. Anyone can make up all kinds of stuff and claim that literally anything could have happened using those kinds of time frames, but the realistic historical time frame for this physical realm is more in the range of 12 – 20,000 thousand years at the longest.

Modern scientists pretend they know exactly how old everything is by using "carbon dating" and other physical methods, but there are so many procedural assumptions involved in carbon dating that the process is scientifically unreliable. Modern processes are foundational to all these cartoonish, spontaneous evolutionary theories, and modern scientists have invested so many finances, so much time, literature, etc., into theories based on carbon dating, that to admit its unreliability now would cause drastic changes, and destroy the very foundations of modern science. God is; men are liars.

Atheists in science like to use natural decay and manifestation rates of matter to produce time/existence estimates for their big bang calculations, but they completely close their eyes to examples of widely varying decay and manifestation rates which happen right in front of us every single day. For example, if I have two bowls of fruit and I put one of them on my kitchen table in July in North Carolina, and the other bowl of fruit in my refrigerator and leave them there for two weeks, one of them is going to rot before the other one, and even a child knows which one that will be.

Decay rates as well as physical manifestations of matter are dependent on many physical variables which each change all the time because everything is in motion. Sometimes physical variables change suddenly and drastically, and at other times the changes are slow and gradual. Physical variables such as changing temperatures, humidity rates, winds, flora and fauna, storms, earthquakes, floods, ice, heat, and other sometimes "catastrophic" events can all quickly change entire environments and ecosystems in ways we are only beginning to appreciate. We are born having no idea what happened before we existed except for what is written in The Word of God and in historical records worldwide. Human beings can only theorize about the past and we can only rely on flawed and skewed "historical records" which are passed along to future generations from most cultures. "Most historical accounts" of histories around the world are only glorifications of whichever culture was in charge at the time. The Truth of The Word of God has never changed and never will.

We should each reexamine our personal "educated speculations" about time, matter, and this universe. All of us need to understand that literally **anything** can happen in a span of even one thousand years. Think about how long that is and how many meteorological and geological changes can occur over a thousand-year period. The Earth has been around much longer than one thousand years, so we can safely deduce that there have been *major* physical changes which have taken place, and that it did not take billions of years for those changes to occur. Accurately identifying the ages of matter based on "established natural decay rates" and modern carbon-dating procedures are replete with flaws and conflicts as far as valid scientific methods are concerned. We are doing our best to try and carnally understand this universe, but without the foundational Truth of God The Creator, it is all foolishness.

The natural rates at which matter forms or disintegrates can be influenced in major ways by natural phenomena much more than we are led to believe by modern scientists. "Scientifically" studying and dating archeological or historical materials based on "standardized rates of deterioration" studies performed under controlled conditions in labs, produces confounded age estimates because in nature, matter deteriorates and manifests at "standardized controlled" rates only for "brief" time periods. Natural processes are far harsher on matter in nature than anything we can partially replicate in experimental labs and then scale up to actual sizes for estimations to be calculated. Human beings cannot replicate the power, dynamics, and effects of large scale, natural environmental processes. We can try and make accurate mathematical and conditional assumptions about processes and consequences, but natural processes can quickly deteriorate or even extend the duration of any matter much faster or slower than we are aware of under variable conditions. Some modern scientists think they know everything, but they will **never** know more than The Creator of it all. How can they? If I manufacture something functional and you're still trying to figure out how it works, how can you know more about that something than I know? It is ridiculous to even think that! God is.

During WWII, German combat forces constructed huge concrete missile facilities in northern France with the intent of firing weapons into England, but the German facilities were bombed into submission by allied forces before they could be used. Those huge, bombed out concrete facilities were subsequently left abandoned for 40 - 50 years and in that "short" time, the natural forests repossessed them all. The concrete structures were so overgrown and completely hidden by the forests that they had to be "rediscovered". The facilities were then excavated and renovated into museums in the late 1990s. This is only one small example of the fact that it does not take millions of years for significant natural changes to occur. Fly Geyser in Nevada for example, only began to form in 1916 (a little over one hundred years ago), and it is already one of the most spectacularly beautiful rock formations to be found anywhere in the natural world. It does not take the Earth's natural geological and meteorological processes multi-millions of years to form nor to destroy anything as atheists want you to believe. My lifetime is nothing compared to only 10,000 years, yet I've witnessed major meteorological and geological changes occur during my short-lived existence….as have you.

We do not "know" for example, how long it took mountain ranges to form, nor for the Grand Canyon to be carved out. Most likely it was carved out by the receding floodwaters of the great flood. We have no idea how long it took for the continents to be separated from each other, nor do we know when that happened. How long did it take for the 7-mile-deep Mariana Trench to form at the bottom of the Pacific Ocean? How about the salt flats in the American state of Utah, or all the unexplored, unexplained underground tunnels and caverns all around the world? Do stalagmites and stalactites sometimes form much faster than "usual", and if so, how much faster (have some of them ever formed overnight or in a week's time)? We can only scientifically speculate about some things, yet modern scientists have convinced themselves that we can explain everything based on a spontaneous, Godless existence.

A worldwide flood draining away as quickly as The Holy Bible describes it did, **fully explains** why we find the Earth's surface and sub-surfaces exactly as we find them today. Stop listening to these devilish scientific liars. If we look at the earth's landscapes (mountains, oceans, piedmonts, valleys, river basins, flood plains, above sea-level and subsurface ponds and lakes, etc.), then a worldwide flood and a "quick" drainage is the **only** explanation. As far north as the expansive island of Greenland is located, a 1966 ice-core study revealed that under the 2-mile-thick ice sheet covering most of the island, there is a one-time layer of sediment between ice levels. The island was completely underwater for a short period of time. There are mummified penguins in Antarctica, and tunnels under the arctic ice with "warmer" ponds and lakes. Entire schools of fish have been fossilized. There are fossilized ocean creatures in various mountaintops all around the world. Even the tallest mountain peak on Earth contains fossilized ocean creatures. There are also different bodies of water (including the oceans) containing "different kinds" of water *within* them all over the world, and each one of the major rivers and their flood basins, glaciers, etc., around the world all clearly indicate that a lot of water drained away quickly in the past at some point, and left the Earth's surface as we find it today. If every word in God's Holy Word is true, then would the world be exactly as it is right now? God is.

Mankind began trying to document time long ago by tracking the sun and its movements. Marking shadows allowed people to track the times of the year so they would know when to plant crops, when the yearly rains were coming, the summer solstice, and all sorts of other things critical to life. Huge stones were arranged in circles which cast the sun's shadows onto indicators at different times of the year so that the people could tell when to do things (what time it was). The oldest known man-made astronomical site on this planet is a Megalithic Stone Calendar called, "Adam's Calendar". This circle of standing stones is in Mpumalanga, South Africa, and is commonly referred to as the "African Stonehenge". This calendar far outdates the more famous Stonehenge in England and many other megalithic structures in existence, and it is STILL functional. The reason the African Stonehenge is barely mentioned in the United States (unlike the European Stonehenge) is strictly racial, and that is a ridiculous shame. Racism is a ridiculous shame, and has been devastatingly harmful to properly understanding this existence.

Mankind constructed early calendars to keep up with times, years, seasons, etc., and the most popular early calendar which was used by many people worldwide was called the Julian Calendar. This calendar was very useful and considered the days and times more closely to what people knew about The Biblical accounts of creation, and the moon's phases, seasons, winds, rains, etc. From the time Jesus Christ was born, people generally began using a new calendar (The Gregorian Calendar) which started from the first year after the birth of Christ and this year was labeled 1AD (Anno Domini; The Year of Our Lord); year number one (1). We began to count the years forward from that point and this separated the time before Jesus Christ was born (Creation; BC years), from the time after His birth ("Anno Domini"; AD). "Before Christ", BC, and "After Death" AD, are easy ways to remember this separation of time, although there are other definitions now which attempt to erase the birth of Jesus from having had anything to do with the time change (yet another evil of modern man).

100

"New" and different calendars have been formulated over the many years since that time, but the modern world still operates by what is called the Gregorian Calendar. The Gregorian Calendar itself has undergone small changes and adjustments since its inception and eventual worldwide acceptance between the late 1500s to 1752. This calendar accounts for leap years and has dropped some days from earlier calendars to make scheduling easier and more accurate for worldwide communication purposes. There are still different calendars in existence around the world which are based on mathematics, astronomical events, cultural themes, religious beliefs, etc., but those calendars have mostly been replaced by the Gregorian Calendar in academic societies so that we can communicate and coordinate with each other more effectively. Everyone is "on the same sheet of music" so to speak.

Because we can identify regularly occurring natural events and document them, we can accurately predict when certain natural events should occur again in the future and therefore make written calendars based on them. Calendars consist of days, months, and years, and we label points and blocks of time such as "2pm", or "17 December through 25 December" for example, to help us coordinate activities worldwide. Even though different cultures of people may sometimes label periods of time differently, we are all still referring to equivalent periods of time. The fact that we can calculate years, months, days, hours, minutes, etc., is a reality because this entire physical existence is finite, and that means that there was a beginning to this physical realm and that there is also an approaching end. We can therefore calculate and measure the beginnings and ends of *everything physical* because everything ***within*** this physical realm has to have begun either "when" or "after" this entire physical realm started, and everything will also end when, or before this physical existence ends.

The fact that everything has a beginning and an end makes it possible for us to physically measure time because time consists of *measurable* spans of moments within this physical realm in which motion takes place. Physical time IS physical motion, and the speed of that motion (from beginning to end) determines the "time" (culmination of the spans of moments) it takes for that motion to have occurred from start to finish. All physical existences are in continuous motion, and this allows us to measure spans of moments (time) because everything's motion is coordinated. That can **only** have been intentionally (and brilliantly) constructed. The *passage* of time in this physical realm is a micro/macro ***continuous*** reality of forces in motion, and every physical thing in existence is in coordinated motion at the molecular level with everything else physical. *Everything* physical is in continuous motion because everything is physically made up of differently combined, continuously moving molecular forces consisting of protons, neutrons, electrons, and other as-of-yet undiscovered charges, forces, and particles. Scientists now believe that dark matter makes up at least 95% of this universe because the physical matter we can sense (see, hear, touch, or otherwise physically detect so far), seems to make up only about 5% of the detectable universal volume.

Motion is what physically binds all matter together and motion in this physical realm is time. Time does not exist without physical motion, so motion is the fabric of physical time/relativity.

Every living human being is a spirit existing in a physical body and because we are constructed as we are, we spiritually recognize that we are physically experiencing the effects of time. Because we are spiritual beings (not subject to physical time) expressing ourselves through our physical bodies (which ARE subject to physical time), then we can independently comprehend the following: When boxers, football players, car accident victims, etc., are physically knocked unconscious, they need to be told later on how much time went by while they were unconscious because they do not know. Every human being who has ever existed has physically gone to sleep and then reawakened virtually oblivious to how much physical time has passed by. In fact, the more physically tired a person is before going to sleep (or the more anesthesia a patient has had for instance), the less spiritually aware they will be of the physical time which has passed when they wake up again. Remember, there is a double-negative correlation between our physical bodies and our spirits sensitivity-wise (hearing, seeing, tasting, smelling, touching). We are existing more spiritually than physically while we are physically unconscious because we are not physically experiencing anything. In spite of our spiritual obliviousness to physical time while we're unconscious, our spirits cannot completely leave our bodies or our bodies will die. A person who is in a coma and on life support systems for example, is not dead because their spirit still remains in their body; they are alive. An otherwise completely healthy body with no spirit/personality in it which is attached to the exact same life support systems is indeed dead. That is only a lifeless body, and this difference is tangible and detectable.

While our bodies are sleeping, we are still spiritually aware of the physical conditions of our bodies and of our immediate environments although to a very diminished extent as compared to when we are conscious. This is demonstrated by a sleeping person's awareness of room temperature changes, uncomfortable body positions, unusual or unexpected sounds and movements in the vicinity, and our bathroom needs. The physical time our bodies experience while we are sleeping or while we are otherwise unconscious (knocked out or in comatose states for example), has zero influence on our spirits because we are not spiritually subject to time. Have you ever gone to sleep and then woke up "a few moments later" only to realize that it had in fact been several hours? We can also go to sleep for what seems to have been a long time, but after we wake back up we realize it has only been a short while. If we experience any sensation of time passing by at all while we are sleeping, then we are still significantly sensing our physical bodies (which are always subject to time), and we are not fully asleep. Our lessened awareness of time while we are unconscious is directly correlated with our level of physical unconsciousness.

Suppose a human being has been dead for 153 years. The passage of time has had *physical* effects on their dead body (decomposition) because that body is still somewhere in this physical realm (probably in a graveyard somewhere). That same time ceased to exist for the spirit which used to occupy that body 153 years ago when that body died because that soul immediately entered the realm of infinity (spirit realm) where there is no such thing as time as we know it. If that same spirit COULD consciously rejoin that same body which had been dead for 153 years (if that person could be reconstituted right now in this physical realm), then "finite time" for that person (that spirit/soul) would start back up again from the exact moment of reconstitution, and that spiritual person (that personality/soul) would have no sense of how much time had physically gone by (153years). They would not have been spiritually subject to it. Again, this is clearly evidenced by unconscious people's obliviousness to how much time has passed since they first became unconscious after they have regained consciousness. We ALL experience this paradigm of timelessness each time we go to sleep and wake back up oblivious to the time which has gone by. This reality also fully explains the scriptures in the Holy Bible which refer to being absent from the body and being present with The Lord (2 Corinthians 5:6-10 KJV), while at the same time saying the dead in Christ shall physically rise first when Jesus comes back (1 Thessalonians 4: 14-17 KJV). Think about that.

What is the spirit realm? What does "eternal", or "forever" mean? The Spirit Realm is literally "forever". God, Jesus, and The Holy Spirit is the Only Existence Who has always been and will always be because God is LITERALLY Infinity. "Forever", "never", "eternity", "always", "ever", "perpetuity", and other such words referencing timelessness all refer to the spiritual realm and realistically speaking, those words should **only** be used during conversations about God or infinity. Fully understanding words referencing infinity is not physically possible for us because we are finite beings. For human beings to try and accurately comprehend anything infinite is impossible without us having The Holy Spirit of God working in us to help us properly understand *infinite concepts* from our finite perspective.

There are spiritual beings *within* the spirit realm right now which are not eternal (the devil and his demons) because they have already been sentenced by God The Creator to eternal damnation; the "second death" (the eternal death of the spirit). That sentence/punishment will be carried out after this entire physical realm ends. We are ALL born knowing that God Is, but we can choose not to believe in God because we have a free will. We can choose to believe whatever we so desire, but the most critical decision each human being makes while we physically exist is, "Do I believe in Jesus Christ (Who is God AND The Holy Spirit) or not?

We are motivated to physically learn to communicate with each other because of our spiritual desires to physically express ourselves to each other. Even those of us who are born with physical challenges develop better and better ways to communicate as time progresses. Because we are finite, physical beings existing in a finite realm, when we try to physically (carnally) understand anything spiritual, we can only hypothesize and formulate theoretical ideas and conclusions based on what we can sense (see, feel, hear, smell, etc.). As a result of this "carnal conclusionizing", mankind has come up with all kinds of misconceptions, mythological concepts, and outright lies concerning the spiritual realm, the physical realm, time, and everything else as well. The spiritual realm is indeed infinite (no beginning and no end) and as far as "time" is concerned, if there is a spiritual equivalent to physical time, then that equivalency is something we cannot possibly physically understand. ONLY The Holy Spirit can help us understand anything spiritual about this physical realm from a Truthful perspective. Any other perspective besides Jesus Christ is unGodly and therefore rooted in mythological, hypothetical, and theoretical lies and confusion. This is exactly where all that big bang/evolutionary foolishness comes from.

Again, it is not possible to physically understand infinity while being finite beings in a finite realm; however, because our spirits are of God (created in His spiritual image and likeness), then we can physically sense *some aspects* of infinity. Close your eyes right now and try very hard to imagine before the beginning of anything physical; when nothing physically existed. There isn't any-*thing* physical anymore including the smallest particle; nothing. Our spirits have a sense of infinity because God Himself (Infinity) is literally our source, so we each spiritually *know* that "forever" exists whether we physically choose to acknowledge that fact or not. Because this finite physical realm was manifested from the infinite spiritual realm, we are physically aware that infinity is a FACT, and the reality of the quantity ("number") zero (0) is one way this can be physically demonstrated. A circle represents the value of "nothing" (infinity), yet it has a physical value which tangibly and consequentially interacts with other physical values, thereby manifesting a physical representation of infinity. Another physical representation of infinity is the mathematical value, "**Pi**" (3.14159265359.....). Pi is calculated as the ratio of the circumference of a circle to that same circle's diameter. This value is absolutely needed for advanced operations in physics, biology, and other scientific genres, and it is a physical representation of an infinite mathematical, foundational constant....nothingness. Pi is a (physical) representation of infinity and just like the number "0", it MUST exist in order for any of the other physical equations to make any applicable sense. God/Infinity is.

Because we are images and likenesses of Infinitely **Perfect** God contained in finite, **imperfect** bodies, then sometimes "glitches" occur. Have you ever been doing something and then suddenly realize that you have been in that *exact* same position before? A powerful realization suddenly hits you that *everything* including *exactly* what is being said (if people are involved) has happened before the exact same way it is happening right now. You KNOW for a fact that you have done this before and then suddenly after only a few seconds, the entire sensation abruptly stops. Afterwards you sit for a few moments trying to figure out what just happened and the realization hits you that it is physically impossible for you to have been in that exact same position before around those exact same people who were saying the exact same things (if people were involved). Even though you know this could not have ever happened before, you still KNOW for a fact that you have been in that exact same position before. I call these "Episodes of Realizations" (ERs), and these are completely different from remembering something or having a "Déjà vu" experience. I will explain the differences in the following paragraph, but these "Episodes of Realization" (ERs) only last for a few seconds and then they abruptly end. "ERs" do not seem to happen to most people, but they are very real occurrences which happen to some people.

Some people mistakenly refer to this sensation as "Déjà vu", but this is not Déjà vu. Déjà vu is; for example, let's say last summer I took a trip to Africa and while I was there I met a beautiful black woman wearing a bright red hat while I was visiting a museum. We instantly liked each other, and we had a great summer together last year. Now, I am in an entirely different African country this summer and two weeks ago I met another gorgeous black woman wearing a bright red hat at a completely different museum. We also instantly liked each other, and we are having a great summer together so far. Now I can look at my new African friend and think to myself, "Now THIS, is Déjà vu". Déjà vu is not an exact reoccurrence of a point in time, but it is when uniquely similar occurrences or situations take place at different times and in different places. This is quite different from a sudden realization that we have been in an exact same moment in time before, and that everything was, and is happening the exact same way. ERs can happen anywhere, and they happen all of a sudden for brief moments and without warning; everything and every word being said is exactly the same to the smallest particle.

As we spiritually exist in these physical bodies which are constantly growing and going through different physical changes, I think imperfections in the connections between our spirits and our bodies happen from time to time in some people. Episodes of Realization (ERs) are the results of deep-rooted juxtapositions between our spirits and our bodies, and right now I am clueless as to *why* it happens or what the associated triggers are for them. I believe that during ERs, people experience a few seconds of separation between their spirits and their physical bodies while they are conscious, and that during these "separations" their *spirits* somehow briefly move forward in time for a few seconds, and they spiritually experience an upcoming moment before they *physically* arrive at that point in time. When they do physically arrive at that moment which they have already *spiritually* experienced, they immediately recognize that point in time and know for a fact that they have experienced that ***exact same*** moment before. It is an unmistakable reality.

ERs are not memories, because memories are stored in our brains and they are recalled from existing storage banks (brain neurons) in different ways. Interestingly, some memories are only recalled when we hear certain music or certain songs being played. Memories recalled by music or songs were probably recorded in our brains while that same music or those same songs were being played. We could have only been thinking about certain songs while certain memories were being recorded and then when we hear those songs again sometime later, detailed memories are stimulated. Have you ever heard a song which unexpectedly took your mind back in time to a particular place or event that you probably would not have remembered otherwise? All kinds of different songs can make all kinds of different people remember all kinds of different things from their pasts.

Hearing particular songs or pieces of music can enrich our here and now environments as well as sometimes spiritually transport us back to particular points in time, but music does not have anything to do with time as far as the *future* is concerned. So, if you'd like to remember an event in detail later in life, play some music; it may help you recall it better sometime in the future. Music is eclectic in its ability to elicit different emotions from people all over the world, while at the same time similarly stimulating and enhancing our brains' abilities to remember all kinds of collateral details which we would not have otherwise remembered. Music has a positive or negative effect on a wide variety of human expressions, emotions, and interactions, and even though there are all kinds of different music and different songs in existence worldwide, it still has the same effects and influences on different kinds of people. Different songs and different music elicit different emotions from people.

Music causes our brains to subconsciously record collateral information in detail, and later on we remember people, places, and events when we hear certain songs again. While we are listening to music or when we hear certain songs, we don't normally consciously say to ourselves, "For the rest of my life whenever I hear this music or this song, it will remind me of this very moment in time." Even if we DO say that, it does not *normally* work out that way. Most of the time when we hear certain music or songs which remind us of past moments, the songs themselves have initiated our memories of past moments which were associated with a time when we were hearing that music or listening to those songs. Song-related memories are almost always subconsciously formed as opposed to having been formed intentionally. Songs can act as spiritual "time machines", and if we could know which songs were playing during particular times in the past, then we could try to get people to remember more details about things we want them to remember.

It is interesting that when we physically visit a place from our past, that place rarely initiates long-lost songs in our minds even if those songs had been playing at the time we were initially in that place; however, songs or music which were playing during times we were initially in certain places, can instantly remind us of those places in detail when we hear those songs again in different places. Songs which do this are mental catalysts for recalling otherwise long-lost memories.

Songs and music initiating memories are quite different from us remembering things we have been taught. Because mankind always tells lies for cultural agendas, then we can only make educated speculations and read between the lines when it comes to the written truth about most things which have happened in the past. When atheists from former times have "officially interpreted" scientific information for people in later generations (us for instance) are left to determine the validity of those interpretations; not the science. This absolutely wastes all kinds of scientific time.

His-story (history) and the truth can be distorted and re-presented as complete lies to future generations, and future generations have no choice but to initially consider those interpretations as historical facts. People were once taught that the world was flat and that the sun goes around the Earth, but there were many more people around the world who always knew better and **never** believed that idea for a second. According to historical records, you would think that everyone used to believe the world was flat until a European taught the world better, and that is just not true at all. Here is an example of how these kinds of things happen: On January 6, 2021, the United States Capitol Building was physically attacked by a Confederate flag-flying mob of violent people after the direct urging of the sitting President of the United States of America, Donald J. Trump. The President's intent was to overturn the results of a legally fair presidential election which he lost. Law enforcement personnel and others were assaulted, seriously injured, and killed, and if various politicians (almost all of them from the Republican Party at the time) had been able to write the official account for the historical records of what happened that day, then later generations would be teaching in their schools that there was a peaceful demonstration at the Capital Building which took place on January 6, 2021 by American-loving Patriots who fought against a "fixed" election, and sought to make sure the votes were being properly counted. That record would have stated that these peaceful Constitution abiding patriots only wanted the US Constitution be followed to the letter as to the election process (which the US Government **was in fact** doing at the time). January 6, 2021 would have ended up being a federal holiday for future generations based on what would have been written in that ridiculously untrue "official historical record".

American children are taught for example, that President Abraham Lincoln never told a lie. I was taught as a child how much he hated slavery, and we teach these things today because it is written in official "historical records"....BUT, most historical accounts of Abraham Lincoln conveniently leave out the fact that he was married to the daughter of the largest slave owner in Kentucky, and that he had slaves himself at times. In 1863 Abraham Lincoln also said about his Emancipation Proclamation (which officially freed the slaves), "…it was a fit and necessary war measure", which speaks to his real motivations because slaves were not going to fight for the ones who are enslaving them against the ones trying to free them. The North needed that manpower and he knew it.

His-storical records also claim that Christopher Columbus discovered America, but he did not even make landfall on the continental United States (as had Africans many centuries before him). When Columbus (and other Europeans) first arrived in the Americas, there were already people here (of African descent) who had obviously been here for several hundreds of years at the very least. Somebody discovered America alright, but it was NOT Christopher Columbus. What about right now? Well, right now "historical records" are claiming that everything came into existence all by itself. "The official scientific interpretation" of our very existence is that because of a spontaneous big bang, all life started all by itself and then evolved from some kind of primordial soup (mud). We are taught that all forms of life on Earth evolved from each other, and that human beings directly evolved from some kind of non-existent chimpanzee after billions of years. These modern "historical records" will teach future generations blatant lies (as has been continuously done in the past). When people discover obvious lies and blatant omissions in "historical records" and attempt to revise them, these revisions are not easily accepted by masses of people because they have been taught so many lies. No human being who has ever existed has ever known they were being lied to until and unless they find out the truth, or they already know the truth and have accepted it. Because the very nature of mankind is physically evil, it has always been difficult for us to accept The Truth about anything. There is always only One Truth about everything, and we exist in an atmosphere of demonic lies (the devil; the author of lying, is here). We are born into sin and shaped in iniquity, but THE Truth is the unchanging God in The Name of Jesus Christ by The Holy Spirit! The Truth has NEVER CHANGED, nor CAN it ever.

Where are we? What are people talking about when they say, "The Universe"? The next chapter is all about this universe and the only way it could possibly exist; yeah, God did it.

(CHAPTER SIX)
OUR UNIVERSE

People everywhere need to be aware that modern scientists are **interpreting** their observations and experimental conclusions almost exclusively through a theoretical big-bang/evolutionary filter. God has proven He created this physical Earth and everything else in existence by the existence of the Earth alone. This is why we are without excuse. All anyone has to do is look around and think for themselves. I am going to list some places all over the Earth which leave no doubt as to God having created this Earth because they are molecularly balanced, spectacularly expansive wonders which all exist at the same time and when we discovered them they were of course, already there.

The Pinnacles – Australia
Antelope Canyon – USA
Kawaijen – Indonesia
Plitvice Lakes – Croatia
Svartifoss waterfall – Iceland
Angel Falls – Venezuala
Marble Caves – Chile
White Desert – Egypt
Teide National Park – Spain
Phang NGA Bay – Thailand
Purnululu – Australia

There are multitudes of other sites, places, wonders, incredible existences, etc., just as spectacular (and even more) as these and to say these are spontaneous, purposeless, pointless, just-happen-to-be-there "things" is just stupid!

Modern mainstream science does not acknowledge the Holy Bible, and they foolishly theorize that the universe spontaneously began as some kind of hot energy tinier than the pointed end of a sewing needle which supposedly somehow held temperatures and/or electrical/KW properties of more than one billion, billion degrees Fahrenheit. This theoretical hot energy mythologically exploded about 10 to 15 billion years ago with a big bang; hence the name of that ridiculous theory.

Atheists theorize that the universe quickly expanded and after only a few seconds, it was already the size of this solar system (about 2,858,307,484 miles wide) and had cooled down to about 10 billion degrees. If this hogwash was even remotely true, then the universe would still be slowing down and cooling off, but instead the universe *manufacturing* all kinds of heat in different places, and it is expanding faster and faster. God is awesome!! Modern astronomers know this, yet they continue to stubbornly hold fast to that spontaneous big bang/evolutionary crap. Atheists say that time, matter, energy, and space, all began with that spontaneous big bang, but if there were no such things as time, matter, energy, and space *before* this mythological explosion, then there would not have been a *moment* for the explosion to have taken place, nor would there have been *anywhere* for it to have happened, and *what was the hot thing composed of* if there were no such things as energy and matter?! God has always been, and God will always be. God is before the beginning of this physical realm, and God is definitely after the end. We, as **finite** beings cannot comprehend infinity. The only explanation for everything (scientific or otherwise) IS that God created everything. God created this universe/time (Genesis 1 KJV; Colossians 1:16-17 KJV; John 1:1-5 KJV; Isaiah 48:12,13 KJV), and based on The Holy Bible and **any** scientific evidence human beings have ever studied, we do not know when that happened. The Truth of The Word of God stands alone and needs no verification from man. Every scientific study in every genre of science has always shown that God created everything, but when modern atheists attempt to *interpret* scientific results, deep confusion always results because Satan is interpreting those results *for* them and they are naturally listening. We are born into sin and shaped in iniquity.

What is this temporary physical realm (the universe)? The universe is **everything** in physical existence **everywhere**. The physical universe is a compilation of continuously interacting micro and macro physical forces partially manifested as mass in a *seemingly* endless vacuum of light and dark energy. Since we can *physically sense* (i.e., see, hear, measure, detect, etc.) the sun, other planets, moons, galaxies, distant stars, etc., then the universe is physical, and is therefore finite. The universe (the entire physical realm) is finite because it has a definitive beginning and a definitive end, and we can sense it with our physical senses.

God placed people on planet Earth and this Earth is part of a "solar system" (planets, rocks, and other matter orbiting around a star) which is estimated to be over 7 billion miles wide. A solar system is made up of a star in the middle (like our sun) with planets (mostly gaseous or rocky) and other physical matter (such as rocks, ice, and dust) going around that star. In our solar system, there are eight (8) officially recognized planets (including the Earth), as well as at least five (5) other "tiny planets" (some of them with moons of their own), large rocks, dirt, ice chunks, etc., orbiting around the sun (a star) in the middle. We call our star in the middle "The Sun". Our sun is a small star as compared to most of the other stars in the universe, and it is only one of over *100 thousand million* stars in our one "small" galaxy. A galaxy is a gathering of billions of individual stars ("suns") and/or solar systems ("suns" with planets going around them) arranged in spirals, ellipticals, and other recognizable patterns and shapes. Most of the stars **in *each*** of the trillions of galaxies out in space are many light years away from each other, and our "little" sun is located somewhere in a relatively small, theoretically spirally shaped galaxy of stars we have named, "The Milky Way Galaxy". I said the shape of the Milky Way Galaxy is "theoretical" because we have never physically seen our galaxy as a whole; therefore, the spiral shape of the Milky Way Galaxy is a scientific speculation/estimation based on cumulative scientific calculations.

From what we can scientifically calculate, the size of the Milky Way Galaxy is almost unimaginably expansive. If we were to get into a vehicle and travel at the speed of light (186,000 miles *each second*), it would still take us at least ***100,000 years*** just to cross this Milky Way Galaxy. After one year of traveling at 186,000 miles each second, we will have traveled about **6 trillion** miles and would still have about 99,999 more years of traveling to go just to cross this one galaxy. To put that into perspective, if you drive a car and you have at least 186,000 miles on your car's odometer, then you can appreciate how long it has taken to register those miles and about how far you have cumulatively traveled. Light travels that far *each second*…yes…each second, light travels 186,000 miles. The size of this Milky Way Galaxy is incredibly immense, and this galaxy seems to be relatively small when compared to other galaxies we can see or detect.

Our Milky Way Galaxy (as large as it is) is only *one* galaxy out of literally trillions of galaxies out in space. There are so many other galaxies in this universe that they are impossible to accurately number, but we estimate that there are literally multi-trillions based on what we can see and detect. As unimaginably huge as **each** galaxy is, they are interestingly grouped into clusters of what seem to be multi-millions of galaxies. *Each cluster* of galaxies is only one cluster in a group of **billions** of other clusters of galaxies from what we can detect and remember, **each** galaxy contains at least one hundred thousand, million stars, some of which are separated by millions of light years. God is FAR beyond incredible! The numbers and the distances involved are mind-boggling and are beyond our physical ability to fully comprehend. In addition to all of that, the galaxy clusters themselves seem to be grouped into *galaxy super-clusters*, and it very literally seems to go on endlessly. It is difficult for us to imagine the distances involved as microscopic as we are, yet we can perceive (sense) the expanse. We absolutely must be little images and likenesses of **The Almighty God** Who created everything, and it indeed takes a place as large as this universe to contain us. God knows what He is doing, and He always has!

The physical universe continues far beyond what we can see and detect with any of our most advanced scientific instruments, and the farther and further out into deep space we investigate, the farther and further out into deep space there is to investigate. Also, our best scientific calculations regarding the size and behavior of this universe seem to come back around onto themselves without any tangible conclusions. For example, Albert Einstein's theories of special and general relativities theoretically explain in understandable ways how the ***large-scale space-time paradigm*** seems to work as far as light and time bending on large scales because of gravity, acceleration, and other electro-magnetic forces (time, speed, and gravity are relative to where you are), but on the other hand, ***tiny-scale quantum physics*** (molecular scale research) seem to indicate that everything (regardless of distances apart) instantly affects everything else (everything is immediately relative to everything else). Those two studies seem to indicate that even though both realities seem to simultaneously exist, they also do not seem to be able to physically coexist as per our current understandings of the laws of physics.

What we DO know is that the manifested matter in this universe we are aware of (galaxies, nebulae, quasars, pulsars, planets, stars, comets, asteroids, moons, etc.) is exquisitely intricately beautiful and incredibly innumerable, and it was all fantastically functioning before we discovered any of it. God knew what it would take to contain us, and every human being should continuously glorify and be in awe of God at the very least, if it's only because of the inexplicable physical wonders He has created! Hallelujah to The Most High!!!!

Modern scientists claim that the universe is almost 14 billion years old because of light/speed calculations based on distant stars which are supposedly located at the theoretical edge of the universe. That "measured distance" is then back calculated at 180 degrees to theoretically account for a complete bubble, thereby supposedly revealing the complete size of the universe. This size/age estimation of the universe is derived from the farthest light sources in deep space we can **currently** detect and the theoretical time it would have taken for that light (which we know the speed of) to have gotten here from those extreme locations. This is one of the ways atheists estimate how long ago the big bang supposedly happened. There are major, major problems with this idea. The better our scientific equipment gets, the more distant stars we continue to detect and this has not stopped. How can an "edge of the universe" be established when there is still space beyond that "edge"? Any historically anecdotal information using any kind of configuration which represents a calculated size of the universe for **any** *"scientific conclusion"* is therefore ONLY circumstantial speculation. Remember that! Be aware that modern scientists commonly use the size of the universe and other related information to bolster their Godless theories as to how we spontaneously came to exist. It didn't happen like that at all. God created ALL of this.

Think about this, if we calculate approximate distances to stars far away from the Earth and then formulate a time the big bang supposedly happened based on how long it has taken light from those stars to get to us, then that is messed up anyway because the light from each star would never have retracted itself from our viewpoint from the beginning since everything supposedly started from the same place. All lights from all the stars would always have been visible from the Earth's perspective, and even if the Earth formed all by itself sometime after the theoretical big-bang (which is ridiculous), then that light would still have been visible when the Earth made itself. If the stars were generated sometime later from a star-making process, then we have no idea when that process took place and therefore, no clue when that light began travelling this way. Because this is true, each star, light, bright spot, etc., would HAVE to have been created and placed wherever it is first, and that is exactly what happened (Genesis 1: 4-8 KJV). When God placed the stars in space, they were immediately visible from the Earth's perspective and they of course, have been ever since.

A spontaneous anything is impossible and what we see out in space are literally zillions of complicated, yet purposely functioning creations (points of light) which are all functioning with God's differently intended purposes. Are we so important to God that He would place us in the center of this seemingly endless physical creation? Yes, we are that important and we are indeed located in the center of this universe.

Everything in deep space is moving away from us from our perspective here on Earth, and since everything in deep space is moving away from us from any observation point on this round planet, then OF COURSE we are at the center of this universe. Think about it, where else could we be?! The Earth is round, and everything in deep space appears to be accelerating away from the Earth from every observation point on this round ball. If we go anywhere on this round ball and look up (out) into deep space and things are moving away from us from every place we look out from, then we absolutely **have** to be in the center of this universe. Again, human beings are the only reason for the existence of anything else physical and yes, we are that special to God. We as individuals *cannot* realize who we are outside of acknowledging The One Who created us in the first place. God in The Name of Jesus Christ by The Holy Spirit created everything. Acknowledging God is truly the beginning of wisdom and understanding about everything and anything, period.

Human beings intentionally organize environments which stimulate desires in our young children to learn more about things by initiating questions in their minds. We do this because we love them more than they can understand and we know more than they do, so we know what they need. We design baby cribs with mobiles, and bedrooms with puzzles, games, maps, and all other kinds of age-appropriate stimulants. We consistently allow our children to discover more and more realities as they mature, and we naturally know how to do this because this is how God has taught mankind.

Suppose one day the children and grandchildren of confessed atheists around the world suddenly decide to believe that their doll babies, soccer balls, and the rest of their toys and possessions spontaneously came from the floors in their bedrooms? Those same kids then begin to curse their parents and start calling them non-existent liars whom they cannot stand. The kids start saying blasphemous things like, "You're not my daddy anyway! I don't have no daddy!", and "*&#@ you mama!" Then big bang/evolutionary atheists would better understand the reality of their relationships with God. Hopefully future generations will change all that kind of foolishness and scientifically respect God more. There are eternally negative consequences for **choosing** to be disrespectfully blasphemous against The Holy, Righteous, Loving, Creator God, so please … STOP THE MADNESS!

Human beings have always been curious about this universe (2 Kings 23:5 KJV), and we know that everything physical is constructed of positive, negative, and neutral forces which are in *continuous motion*. Motion is a physical property which *everything* in this physical realm shares, and this means that everything in this physical realm has a force relationship (in varying degrees) with everything else in this physical realm (quantum entanglements). Because motion is a common property in everything physical (micro and macro), then coffee tables, photons, automobiles, comets, footballs, moons, crayons, stars, planets, paint cans, galaxies, etc., are all inter-connected in this ultra-magnetic, electro-chemical, gravitational vacuum we call the universe. Scientific Special and General Relativity study results are only beginning to scratch the surface when it comes to helping us understand some of the deeper aspects of force/motion relationships.

Our sun is very hot. The average temperature across the surface of the sun at any given time is about 7,600 degrees Fahrenheit (F); that is extremely hot. Sometimes "cooler" areas mysteriously appear and disappear in circular shapes in different locations across the surface of the sun and we call these "sunspots". Sunspots tend to range in temperature from around 4,600 degrees F at the "coolest", to around 7,500 degrees F, and because these circular areas are cooler than the sun's surface around them, they appear to us as dark spots. For reasons yet unknown, sunspots increase in number about every 11 years and when this happens, it causes a tiny decrease in the sun's overall temperature of only about 1/10th of 1 degree. This ever-so-slight temperature change significantly affects the Earth's weather and its magnetosphere and causes all kinds of different storms to occur worldwide. The Aurora Borealis (electromagnetically initiated lights across the northern skies) near the Earth's polar regions also significantly increase. The Earth is approximately 93 million miles from the sun, and it takes light and the other energies the sun expels (solar winds, north and south magnetic waves, photons, electromagnetic radiation, electricity, heat, gamma rays, etc.) around 7 minutes to reach the Earth.

Scientists believe the sun's "gravitational pull" holds all the planets (even the "little planets" beyond Pluto) in stabilized orbits around it. It takes over three hours moving at the speed of light (186,000 miles *each second*) to get to Pluto from the sun. That is a long way, and it would take a ***very strong*** gravitational pull alone to hold celestial bodies in disciplined orbits from those extreme distances. This is why I

LINDSEY K. HAM SR.

believe the sun's gravitational pull is only part of the equation when it comes to planetary orbital consistencies.

If our sun was the size of a basketball, then Pluto would get almost an entire mile away from that basketball during its orbit and Pluto would be about the size of one of the tiniest grains of sand from any beach compared to that basketball. There are obviously other forces keeping the sun's orbiting matter from either being sucked into it (Mercury, Venus, and the Earth), or from being released out into space (Uranus, Neptune, Pluto, etc.). Because there are natural variations in everything physical, then surely after at least 10,000 years of physical existence, *something* would have naturally affected at least some of the gravitational pulls enough to have caused either of those changes to have taken place (planets sucked into the sun or released out into space). Dark matter energy, gravity, and electro-magnetic forces regulate planetary disciplines when it comes to their orbital paths.

I believe there is *an electromagnetic repulsion and simultaneous attraction* of each planet coming from the sun. This, combined with each planet's motion around the sun is what is keeping each planet in the orbits they are in. There is a giant south and north pole of a "magnet" in the sun which is uniquely repelling and attracting at the same time, the north and south poles of *each* planet. This magnetic force in the sun flips around every eleven (11) or so years (the north pole of the sun's "magnet" becomes the south pole and vice-versa) and this is making the repulsion/attraction of each planet happen. This, along with the orbital and rotational speeds of each planet ensures that each planet stays true to its pathway around the sun. It is all balanced. God is supremely intelligent, and there are NO WORDS to describe His glory. Every molecule of this entire creation is solid proof that The

Creator God is, because everything is purposefully balanced and functioning. This is why we are "without excuse". The "fear" (respect) of The Lord is the beginning of wisdom (Proverbs 1:7; 9:10 KJV), (Psalm 111:10 KJV) and people shamefully disrespect God every single time they **foolishly** ascribe His glorious masterpiece (this universe) to some "pointless spontaneous occurrence".

Some people believe this "pointless spontaneous occurrence" (the big bang and evolution) also supposedly produced more intelligent life forms than human beings; "aliens". These aliens supposedly navigate all the way through interstellar space in advanced starships to come to the Earth from distant worlds, only to fly into the Earth's atmosphere and streak across the sky in UFOs (Unidentified Flying Objects). That is laughably ridiculous. Incredibly intelligent alien species with big heads flying to the Earth in "UFOs" (Unidentified Flying Objects) do not exist anymore than "Santa Clause" or "Mickey Mouse" does; but angels and demons do. I'm pretty sure you can guess which one of those entities is behind people claiming to have been in the presence of big-headed aliens from UFOs. That being said, there are indeed mysterious interactions with angels which have taken place in mankind's history according to the Bible and those interactions suggest that there is a whole lot we can still learn about this physical existence. What we know is that spontaneity is purposeless and that it could not intricately design a physical realm which we factually know *completely* functions with and for many purposes. **Everything** in existence has God-given purposes so the entire idea of a pointless, Godless existence makes no sense at all under any circumstance.

Motion is common in everything physical because everything physical is in motion at the molecular/subatomic level at varying speeds. Molecular scientists correctly believe that atoms (as we have chosen to call them) are tiny individual collections of *specifically arranged* positive, negative, and neutral forces, and that *the amount* of each of those individual forces present in each atom determines what kind of physical element (matter) each atom will help to manifest when it's combined with other atomic forces. We think that weak atomic combinations of these forces manifest soft matter such as cotton, feathers, grass, etc., while tighter/stronger combinations of those same forces (covalent bonds for example) help manifest hard matter such as rocks, iron, diamonds, etc. Again, atoms are believed to be tiny combinations of positive, negative, and neutral forces, and there are theoretically multi-trillions of atoms making up any small area of anything physical. Into all that spectacular brilliance, God infused intricate audio-visual processes which add sounds and colors to the atomic combinations which manifest matter. He obviously did that to artistically enhance our existence in this physical realm. Hallelujah!

We think matter is composed of combined forces of energy (atoms) and if this is true, then theoretically we should be able to make existing matter disappear or fall apart by dis-integrating the atomic bonds which make up that matter (suddenly remove the protons, electrons, or neutrons and store them). We should also be able to make that same matter reappear again by re-pressuring those same dis-integrated atoms back together (reintroducing the stored protons, electrons, or neutrons back to the atoms we got them from) exactly as they were before. If we are eventually able to do this, we would then be able to predict disintegration/manifestation pressures, and therefore control when we disintegrate or manifest anything. Atheists in the scientific community will then undoubtedly try and use that discovery/ability to further disrespect God by then claiming that this proves that matter could have been spontaneously manifested; however, there is NOTHING spontaneous about the processes I've just described. It still takes an external force to disintegrate or manifest anything physical, and the disintegration/reintegration tool itself would have to be constructed from already existing matter. There is nothing spontaneous about any of that, so the exact same question persists for atheists. Where did The Force causing all matter to manifest come from in the first place?

The spontaneous processes atheists describe which supposedly started this entire physical existence could not have happened. The fact that physical materials are needed to try and initiate a theoretically spontaneous God-particle (Higgs-Boson) which supposedly initiated everything physical, means that it could not have happened spontaneously anyway. Think about it. Everything is purposed. To every action there is some kind of reaction, but there must first be an action. Everything was created for many purposes and again, spontaneity literally means "without purpose". It is a scientific fact that there is no such thing as "spontaneity", so why then do modern scientists continue to claim that everything is spontaneous? It is all demonic and should make no sense to anyone; especially supposedly intelligent people.

Mankind's attempts to prove a spontaneous beginning is one of the motivations behind constructing High-Energy Particle Accelerating Machines around the world, such as the underground CERN (European Organization for Nuclear Research) particle physics laboratory (Large Hadron Collider) located near Geneva, Switzerland. It is a large underground tube approximately 17 miles in circumference and is buried about 574 feet underground. It is packed full of extremely powerful, ultra-sensitive electromagnetic configurations which are used to accelerate molecular forces at or near the speed of light and then it smashes them together for the purpose of discovering evidence of a particle which scientists call a "God-particle", or "Higgs-Boson". This theoretical inevitability (Higgs-Boson) supposedly helped initiate the spontaneous big bang "creative explosion" which fortunately for everything in existence (tisk, tisk), brought forth all this perfectly interacting, **purposeful** physical matter for no reason at all. Stop it.

At some point in 2012, a Higgs-Boson particle was reportedly discovered at this facility, but of course this "discovery" has not been shown to have spontaneously initiated anything and it never will show anything even close to that. Nothing has ever happened spontaneously, and since we have to smash physical particles (photons) together to try and initiate a "spontaneous particle" which supposedly created purpose, then how could that particle have been spontaneous from the beginning if we can make it? None of that makes any sense. Energy has always existed, and that Continuously Existing Energy (which atheistic scientists are always attempting to physically identify) *is*, has *always been*, and *always will be*; God.

If we can reproduce anything, then it **could not** have been spontaneous. All we **ever** do in science is **discover** more and more **already existing** physically stable, obviously pre-designed forces which have existed since creation. Everything we discover, test, or whatever we do with it, was already there long before we found/discovered it and yep, God did it. "Scientific misinterpretations" from CERN study results are being used to try and validate modern atheistic theories. The

Higgs-Boson has nothing to do with spontaneously creating anything. If a Higgs-Boson is a catalytic, energy converting particle which God created in the beginning to assist in the manifestation of matter, then so be it; but the Higgs-Boson (nor any other particle) did not create itself any more than that lightbulb in your ceiling did. If I take a piece of flint rock and strike it against another rock and a spark results, does that mean the spark spontaneously created the flint and the other rock because the resulting fire is a different element than either of the rocks? Of course not, but unfortunately this is how modern scientists are thinking, and is absolutely ridiculous.

Atheistic explanations for the Higgs-Boson and other force/particle *discoveries* must be explained the way they are being explained to the world so that they can fit into already existing, demonic misinterpretations of scientific data. God created EVERYTHING, so whatever we "discover" was already here and we only investigate the purposes of things we discover. We investigate things to find out their purposes because we already KNOW that everything has purposes. Again, spontaneity means without purpose, and when we do not understand the purposes for things, we misuse, abuse, or misapply those things until we eventually recognize their intended (by God) purposes and how they can be useful to us.

Do not be mislead. ***Everything*** discovered during particle acceleration-collision studies or at any other modern scientific facility or platform (including deep space observations from the James Webb, Edwin Hubble, or other even more advanced systems and telescopes) will ALWAYS reveal that everything has been designed by God and is functioning with His pre-designed purposes. It takes a "room" the size of this universe to contain human beings, and in Chapter 7, "*Modern Science vs. The TRUTH About the Universe and Organic Existences*", I will go into even more details about why modern scientific confusion occurs when trying to atheistically explain this universe.

(CHAPTER SEVEN)
MODERN SCIENCE VS. THE TRUTH ABOUT THE
UNIVERSE AND ORGANIC EXISTENCES

There can be night and day differences between the interpretations of "scientific results" and "The Truth". What is "Science"? What is this process which modern people worship and trust so much? Is "Science" some kind of independent force which can be studied (Scientology)? What meanings can science produce, and who is officially interpreting the results? What is "Science"?

"Professional Science" is a trusted method mankind uses to investigate and attempt to understand God's **physical** creations so that we can develop valid conclusions about them. Human beings have come to *objective* scientific conclusions about many physical things over time, but *our interpretations* of the results of scientific investigations are *subjective*, and this is an inherent problem. It seems that most modern scientists are presenting their interpretations of investigative results to the world through big bang/ evolutionary/atheistic filters, and what is happening in science today is a shame. Professional science in every genre of study clearly shows that God created this universe, and the scientific processes we use are reliable enough for us to produce truthful answers to scientific questions. The following steps are a basic description of the "scientific method":

1. We observe the curiosity/subject of study and document those observations
2. We formulate particular questions about the curiosity (we develop hypotheses)
3. We make predictions about what the answers to those questions will be
4. We gather the relative equipment to construct the experiments which will hopefully answer the questions

and allow for experimental replication to validate the results

5. We perform the test/experiment/procedure/examination

6. We objectively interpret the results and either accept or reject the hypotheses

Because scientific investigation results are now being subjectively interpreted by influential individuals through atheistic filters, a significant percentage of **flawed** "scientific conclusions" are being presented to the world as if they are verified facts. Atheistic scientific interpretations are only theoretical ideas and misguided assumptions, and THIS is what perpetuates most of the modern problems between Holy Bible believers (the church) and modern scientists. The spontaneous big bang explanation for the beginning of everything (including life) is by far the most prominent example of the modern scientific community intentionally and aggressively presenting (what they know to be) false conclusions to the world in the name of "science" with the obvious intent of trying to disparage the Truth of the Holy Bible. Studying physical matter helps us better understand physical facts, but when people do not acknowledge **The Creator** of that matter, then understanding the truth about that matter is not possible. There are **zero** conflictions between The Word of God and science, but "the world" (the devil) tries to twist the Truth into a lie by interpreting science **for** the world through atheistic filters (Proverbs 3:5-6 KJV) (Proverbs 14:12 KJV).

Why should anyone believe that God created this universe and how can we possibly know the truth about any of that? We do not *naturally/physically* know the truth about anything because we are physically born into sin and environmentally shaped by evil, which is the antithesis of Truth (Psalm 51:5 KJV). Remember; it is impossible for you to know you are being lied to unless you either already know the truth, or you accept the truth later on after having been presented with it. Because we do not initially know the truth about anything, we investigate everything, and we are driven to discover physical purposes for matter (why?). What drives us is that we already KNOW that there are many purposes for each form of matter. We desire to know "Why?" because "Why?" is an inquisition *about purpose* initiated by our already existing spiritual knowledge that there are many purposes for everything in existence. We each inherently KNOW in our hearts that a spontaneous, purposeless existence is impossible, but we can choose to say we believe whatever we desire. Remember, "science" is only a *physical system* we use so that we can better understand physical matter, but *the reality of God having created everything* is literally *the interpretation* of physical matter.

Without righteous interpretations of scientific research, physical "conclusions" continuously change over time because they are not rooted in Truth. The Spiritual Truth (God) has NEVER changed, and The Spiritual Truth NEVER will. The exact same written Words from God our ancestors had, we have right now. The way things are done (technologically) in this "modern age" is not the only way for humanity to exist, and this generation is vain enough to think that we are the smartest and "most advanced" humans to have ever existed. We don't know what prior civilizations were doing technologically, but it is very clear that they were doing and building things we cannot do and build today. It is also very clear that they were much more respectful to God The Creator than people are now.

Of course it takes faith to believe that God created everything because God does not have to prove ANYTHING to us. He has already done that. **Salvation is about faith** in The Truth, and since **every** single word in The Word of God is true, then the world is exactly as it is right now. As Jesus said on the cross, "It is finished." It literally takes demonic rebellion to believe that everything is spontaneous and meaningless because how can anyone believe this all happened by itself when molecularly balanced, inanimate and organic existences have always been functioning with many unquestionably designed purposes? It is absolutely ridiculous to think that everything is happening on its own for no reason. Everything is NOT spontaneous, meaningless stardust with no purpose. ALL of that mindset is authored by the devil because we ALL KNOW that each and every little thing exists for many purposes (Psalm 14:1 KJV).

If this existence was spontaneous, then there could be no such thing as consistency. Anything would happen at any time for no reason because of spontaneous chemical changes. Nothing could be predictable. Sometimes a stick of dynamite would explode as expected because of the timed detonator, and at other times that stick of dynamite would suddenly turn into an old basketball with grass growing out of it, or a cone of metamorphic rock with an inflated bicycle tire in it. Anything would suddenly turn into something no person has ever seen before at any time, and brand-new elements would still be spontaneously coming into existence.

God obviously created every ingredient which makes up this entire physical universe (Genesis, Hebrews 11:3; KJV),

LINDSEY K. HAM SR.

but God; The Almighty Creator, is rarely acknowledged (if at all) in contemporary science. In The United States of America, the **modern** idea of excluding God from anything scientific is perpetuated by intentionally misapplying the United States Constitution's First Amendment. Scientists in the United States try to use the First Amendment to justify leaving God out of anything scientific by claiming it demands a "separation of church and state"; however, the First Amendment to the United States Constitution does not outlaw documenting the truth. The First Amendment literally states that: "Congress shall make no law respecting an establishment of religion, or prohibiting the free exercise thereof; or abridging the freedom of speech, or of the press; or the right of the people peaceably to assemble, and to petition the government for a redress of grievances."

What does that mean when it comes to scientific investigations? What that means as far as "separation of church and state" is that the government of the United States of America **will not make any "religious" laws**, nor dictate anything to anyone about who they worship, how they worship, what they worship, when they worship, nor anything else regarding "religion". The First Amendment to The United States Constitution has NOTHING at all to do with scientists acknowledging The Truth they find out about during scientific research. The Truth is The Truth and lies and omissions are lies and omissions. Modern scientists completely disregard even the mention of God The Creator in anything, yet they are quick to mention things like, "mother nature", "karma", "natural selection", "universal force", "luck", "gods " of this and that, "mythological beliefs", "spontaneity", "fingers crossed", "happenstance", "just happened to...", etc.

God is, and those are only replacement words for The Almighty coming from people who recognize that God is, but do not want to acknowledge The Creator. Please understand; there is only One Truth, but there are all kinds of different religions, lies, beliefs, and atheistic explanations. Atheistic denials and confusion reign in these last days of mankind, and God will not tolerate this level of disrespect too much longer.

I am in full agreement that there should indeed be a "separation of religions and state", but this is completely different from a "separation of TRUTH and state". There should be a THICK wall between "religions" and "state" (official scientific investigations), because "Religions" and The Truth are two different things most of the time, but The Truth is ALWAYS The Truth. There are all kinds of different religions, and different religions believe all kinds of different things; but there is only "One Truth". Who among us can determine what the truth is about anything? Well, we have already been told The Truth, and when we scientifically investigate matter and factual truths about that matter are revealed, then why would any "professional scientist" deny what the science clearly shows? Science *clearly* shows that God created this universe because *everything* we have discovered was already functioning with *intelligently designed purposes* when we discovered it; everything has been and everything always will be. There is nothing we have ever discovered which spontaneously came into existence and has no meaning...nothing. Any engine in any car for example, is an obviously intentionally designed, complicated functioning part of that car which produces power to turn the wheels so the car can move. As complicated and obviously intentionally designed as different car engines are, it is ridiculous for anyone to believe that any engine in any automobile anywhere suddenly designed, and then put itself together. That would be absolute foolishness, and we all know this. God's creations (organic and inorganic) are so much more complicated than the most complicated engine, that it isn't even worth wasting the time to compare them, so how much more foolish are those people?

The **purposefully designed** structure of this universe should be scientifically acknowledged. Science does not and cannot validate "religion", but it has **always** validated The Truth of God's creation. God, Jesus, nor The Holy Spirit will **never need** any verification from man. When scientists investigate things and those investigations directly line up with what is written in The Holy Bible, then those scientists should be able to publicly acknowledge The Word of God. Science has ALWAYS proven every single Word of The Holy Bible, but because the spirit of the anti-Christ is in this world and we are all born and raised into this physical realm of confusion and blasphemy, then *worldly* modern scientists intentionally lie, theorize, and hypothesize **against** The Holy Bible as much as possible. This does *not* happen for scientific reasons; it is strictly spiritual. Resistance to the Truth only verifies that the devil exists because the folks putting up those resistances to The Truth (modern scientists) are far and away smart enough to know better.

All of us have sense enough to know that we are only *discovering* already ongoing functions, purposes, and processes, and we are almost continually *discovering* new things (atomic elements, neutrinos, dark matter, matter, forces, particles, quarks, etc.). Either these things are already fulfilling their God-designed purposes in the quantum physics field when we discover them, or they are spontaneous purposeless things which just luckily perfectly fit into the workings of everything in existence. If things are spontaneous, then there could not be any such thing as functional consistency. If elements spontaneously came into existence, they would still change at any given time and there would be unimaginable effects on the stability of everything; nothing could coexist.

"Science" is a beautiful, very important activity and because of it we can collectively learn all kinds of truths about this physical realm; however, this new idea of "science" being some sort of creative force to be worshipped, or science itself being something we can study (Scientology) is absurd. It is madness. The existences of anything new we discover have nothing at all to do with "science" except that they were **discovered** via scientific processes. Again, science is only a process by which human beings professionally learn about what God has already created and if atomic forces are only "spontaneous things", then there would be no purpose for them, and they could not *consistently* fulfill the purposes they do. Because we do not understand the purposes of various ongoing functions, this in no way gives modern scientists green lights to ascribe spontaneous existences to them.

Foolish ideas such as the theoretical existences of alternate universes accessible by wormholes (which have supposedly existed forever), and claiming that all life forms are currently transitional species in different stages of becoming something else are the results of false interpretations of science. There is no science which verifies ANY of these kinds of intentionally misleading theories and demonic imaginations. None of those kinds of Hollywood fantasies agree with The Word of God, and none of them are scientifically verifiable, so they are all therefore, fantastic LIES. The tangible **facts** in this physical existence all verify The Word of God, so do not allow yourselves to be fooled. God is.

If modern scientists from any discipline include anything about God in any of their research explanations or conclusions, then the information is "professionally disregarded" by the modern scientific community and then government or other funding is normally discontinued. This has caused major interpretational confusion when it comes to explaining scientific results because scientists are afraid to publish The Truth they discover. We all know that God is because nothing begins from nothing, and scientifically discovering already purposefully functioning processes speaks for itself. Everything has to have been created.

The fact that human beings naturally/physically resist acknowledging the obvious spiritual Truth of God in Jesus' Name is solid proof that we are spirits of God in physical bodies literally *made from* this demonically defiled physical earth which has already been sentenced to eternal damnation. This is what salvation is all about. The anti-Christ (the devil) spiritually exists in this physical realm, and (it) always tries to negatively influence each of our spirits to be physically blasphemous. We are each naturally intelligent enough to know that God HAS TO EXIST, and when spiritual and physical Truths are presented to people who are intelligent enough to understand them, yet they continuously position themselves against those truths, then there HAS to be a negative spiritual influence behind that position, otherwise, why else would that happen? The devil **IS** that negative spiritual influence and he is not some joker in a red suit tossing people into hell with a pitchfork. The devil is an anti-God, spiritual influence existing in this physical realm who has already been sentenced to eternal damnation. He does not have to toss anyone anywhere because those who choose to go along with the devil by resisting Jesus

Christ, have already made a conscious decision to follow the devil into eternal damnation.

Anything *physical* can be manipulated (changed, defiled, deformed, rearranged, made better or worse, etc.) and as a reminder, all of God's organic creations (life forms) *make* things from what God has already *created*. To "create" something literally means to make something out of nothing, and to "**make**" something means to take already created elements and change them. God created every physical ingredient which makes up this entire universe (including all life), and since the time of creation, God's created organisms have made things by combining and changing the already created variables. Precisely organized, extremely mathematically perfect, chemically balanced, stable physical existences which could only have been "created", are always everywhere around us in micro and macro forms. If this existence was spontaneous then NOTHING would nor could be stable or predictable. Nothing could be consistent.

Scientists say that the universe seems to be expanding based on observations and different tracking systems in different places around the Earth. The Bible refers to the "outer space" we can see, study, and enter as "the heaven", or "heavens". For example, Psalms 8:1; KJV states, "O Lord our Lord, how excellent is thy name in all the earth! Who has set thy glory *above* the heavens". This tells us that God is bigger than the universe, and of course this is true because He created it! It seems logical that the border/edge of the universe (wherever that is) is the edge of this physical realm and where it meets God's Pure Spiritual Glory (Infinity). This entire universe is encapsulated by Spiritual Infinity. God is everywhere at the same time, and He always has been, and He always will be. Even though we cannot comprehend that, we DO have a

143

sense of eternity, and we can spiritually sense God in The Name of Jesus Christ.

God placed the stars, the Earth, the sun, the moon, the planets, and other physical matter in outer space where they are and then set everything motion, and one of the most interesting things He did was to include big-bang/evolutionary "impossibilities" in His creation. He did these things because God of course, knew exactly what the spirit of the anti-Christ (the devil) was going to try and eventually do in the evil, foolish, gullible, and sin-filled minds of modern man. For example, the planet Neptune's largest moon (Triton) orbits Neptune in the opposite direction from the rotation of the planet (a retrograde orbit which causes drag, friction, and heat), yet that moon is the **coldest matter** in this solar system. There are *more* moons in this solar system which orbit their planets in opposite directions as well, and none of this would have been spontaneously possible by any of the "laws of physics" (which were established by God). God did that and many more things to destroy any foolishness about spontaneity.

There is no justification for believing in a spontaneous existence. Another example is the planet Uranus which is positioned on its "side" and is rotating sideways in relationship to its orbit around the sun. It's "North Pole" is pointing at the sun which is different from any other planet. There are trillions of spontaneous beginning "impossibilities" God has designed into this universe and most of them are blatantly obvious. Matter in deep space is moving AWAY FROM US faster and faster instead of slowing down had there been a theoretical big bang. Big bang theorists claim that the big bang eventually began to slow down (as it naturally eventually would) as it dispersed from its initial imaginary spontaneous explosion, yet universal expansion is increasing in speed.

If we could study this solar system from above, we would see that all of the planets are going around the sun on a plane in a counterclockwise direction, and the *individual rotations* of most of the planets are also counterclockwise. It is as if they are rolling around the sun, but there are two exceptions. One of them is a very large gas planet located very far away from the sun (Uranus), and the other planet is small and rocky, and located extremely close to the sun (Venus). Uranus is rotating clockwise, while Venus seems to be positioned upside down causing it to rotate clockwise as well. Venus is the slowest spinning matter in the known universe. Jupiter is by far the largest planet in our solar system, and it is large enough to contain all the other planets *as well as* all of the other matter going around the sun, yet it rotates (spins around) much faster than any of the other planets. Modern astronomers say Jupiter is a large ball of very light gasses which spins as fast as it does because it is conforming to the "rules" and "laws" of physics; yet we have filmed rocks and debris "physically impacting" that big ball of light gasses. Interesting.

Atheistic scientists come up with demonic ideas by any means necessary to counter The Holy Bible, and please do not ever forget that. There is God and there is the devil; make your choice. The Holy Bible (The Word of God) very clearly explains exactly how this physical realm came to be, and I detailed this in the Creation Chronology on page 4. Remember this; all rules, laws, directives, instructions, etc., are **intentionally** put in place by whoever is in charge, and this includes the rules and laws of physics, quantum-physics, heat, gravity, thermodynamics, meteorology, oceanography, geology, and any other "ology", whenever, and wherever. God did it.

Atheists conjure up demonic ideas such as sister universes, alternating dimensions, fantasy worm-hole theories, and all kinds of other made-up crap to try and imply that physical time, energy, matter, and space have always existed. The problem is that none of that mess is scientifically supportable and none of those things are physical realities we observe, study, nor have documented at any time. There is not one shred of scientific evidence to support ANY of the modern atheistic fantasies. None of them line up with The Holy Word of God, so do not believe all these devilish lies out here which run counter to the Biblical account of creation. Anyone can come up with all kinds of theoretical "conclusions" if they are given multi-billions of years to play with, and then they can find statistical data they can manipulate to make it seem to support whatever they want to say. This is modern science. The devil is here and he is the author/father of lies, so of course this is how the atheistic modern scientific community operates. Willful, spiritual ignorance is inexcusable, and it is blasphemy of The Holy Spirit because a person is calling God a liar when they believe in that big bang/evolutionary evil foolishness.

Regardless of their states of being (solid, liquid, gas, plasma, or whether they are cold or hot, etc.), elements remain being what God created them to be. We can make reliable predictions about each chemical's behavior as well as their reactions to other chemicals under all kinds of variable conditions because God created each element to be exactly what it is and to maintain the properties He gave each one. We know that elements do not spontaneously change. If elements were spontaneous, then they would suddenly change because they couldn't be stable, and new elements would still be coming into existence. It would be impossible for us to exist as we do.

Because God created everything with purposeful stability, we can make millions of plastic jars of different tasting peanut butters for example, because we KNOW that if we mix particular ingredients together in particular ways with particular amounts of each ingredient, then unique tasting peanut butters will reliably result. We can put different kinds of peanut butter in differently manufactured jars *knowing with confidence* that there will be no cross-contamination from the jars, and that the jars will not spontaneously change into something we have never seen before.

How is chemical stability possible at all if chemical elements are only the results of "spontaneous happenings" at the atomic level? Each chemical, each molecule, each atom, force, etc., could not be able to maintain any stability if they were only spontaneous happenstance. Surely at least some of the elements would still be changing into something else every now and then. Each jar of peanut butter for instance, would spontaneously develop its own taste, smell, texture, etc. Sometimes the jars would hold the peanut butter and sometimes they would not. The jars, the labels on the jars, or the peanut butter in the jars could suddenly catch on fire, or turn into leaves, or become earwax at any moment because of unforeseen spontaneous chemical changes. Anything would happen to anything anywhere at any time if this physical existence was spontaneous. Don't believe the lies! Everything has been purposed by God Almighty.

According to atheists, shortly after everything began all by itself, the universe continued to spontaneously expand and huge gas clouds of hydrogen and helium atoms appeared out of nowhere and *made themselves* into unimaginably complex stars and galaxies. The stars and galaxies then *organized themselves* into the galaxy clusters and super-clusters and patterns we find out in space today. They say that within each galaxy, trillions of stars and planets *formed on their own* and *then gathered themselves* into complex, organized orbits, rotations, and recognizable patterns. Not only did the hydrogen, helium, and other elements *decide to form into shapes and patterns* recognizable to human beings, but nebulae, quasars, pulsars, and all kinds of other matter out in space also *decided they would form on their own* and *place themselves wherever they wanted to be.* Some of them even "decided" to form into shapes of manufactured and organic things way back here on Earth like rings, horses heads, hands, etc.

The Earth then *formed all by itself and decided to get* perfectly far enough away from the sun for everything to start working perfectly. Then the Earth perfectly *tilted itself* 23 degrees towards the sun and *decided to settle itself* into a perfect orbit. The Earth then *decided to spin* at a perfect rotation speed so that days, years, seasons, water, life, etc., could all spontaneously appear. When life started all by itself, it spontaneously developed into perfect co-existences, and some life forms even evolved to be prey for other animals to specifically eat. Go figure.

There is no "scientific" explanation for the moon. If the moon suddenly ceased to exist, then all life on Earth would be in immediate catastrophic trouble and the sun would initiate immediate devastation to all life on Earth. The Earth itself would drastically change because everything would either freeze, burn up, float off into space, and all life would die in a poisoned, magnetically, electrified atmosphere. God positioned everything so that the moon **perfectly** eclipses the sun and only the sun's outer atmosphere (the corona) is visible during perfectly designed eclipses. Our moon is the only moon in existence which is calculated to be so perfectly distanced from its planet that it produces perfect eclipses. That is intentionally intricate precision. According to atheists, this happened all by itself! God also perfectly coordinated the moon's rotation, orbit, and other forces to cause the same side of the moon *to always face the Earth*, and we call this tidal synchronization. Even though the Earth and the moon are different sizes and they are each rotating, the same side of the moon always faces the Earth. Just think about the mathematical precision involved in creating that. Yep; only God could have done that.

Try to imagine The Awesomeness it takes to create two round, differently sized balls levitating in the most extremely hostile and lifeless atmosphere in existence, with each ball having its own independent sphere of gravity. God made each ball rotate at different rates of speed (because they are different sizes) and made the smaller ball (the moon) orbit around the larger one (the Earth) while keeping the same side of the moon always facing the Earth. God positioned everything so that the sun is perfectly and predictably eclipsed by the moon when viewed from the Earth's perspective. The moon also causes various changes all over the surface of the Earth, most notably the critical oceanic tides. Hallelujah!! God Is Supreme Intelligence far beyond our abilities to understand. The moon produces tides in the oceans and seas all over the world while appearing from the Earth to be in different phases (full, half, new, etc.). Think about it all. The same side of the moon always faces the Earth, yet the Earth and the moon are each continuously spinning at their own rates of speed as the moon goes around the Earth, while the Earth is going around the sun. This is only one tiny aspect of the awesomeness of God's physical creations. God is!!!

The moon's effects occur so regularly that we can produce dependable schedules and calendars from those predictable effects, but the moon is also moving away from the Earth a tiny bit each year. Not that the moon was ever in contact with the Earth but if it ever was, then moving away at the rate it's moving, it would have been in contact with the Earth anywhere between 9000 to 14,000 years ago (allowing for motion variations and other possible anomalies). What God has done is absolutely amazing! There are no such things as perfect "spontaneous coincidences" because there's no such thing as spontaneity...lies...all lies. God created perfect physical equations and all kinds of corresponding matter manifests that. Do you know that if you lined up every single planet in this solar system (including Pluto), that they would just about perfectly fill in the distance from the Earth to the moon. The moon is about 238,900 miles from the Earth, so could this be spontaneous happenstance? Of course not. Atheists have no explanation for the moon's existence anyway, except to say that maybe an asteroid about the size of Mars struck the earth sometime in the past and knocked a chunk of the Earth out into space and that became the moon (stop laughing). There are *too many* common sense reasons why this theory and others like it are absolutely preposterous. Did this happen only a few thousand years ago? Could this be what happened to the dinosaurs? Did Santa Clause have anything to do with this?! Peter Pan?!

The existences of any of the moons around any of the planets in our solar system cannot be explained without God having created them. Each moon orbiting each planet (some planets have many moons, and some have none) is characteristically very different from the other ones. There are about 180 (+) moons that we know of orbiting the eight (8) large planets and (5) five smaller "dwarf planets" in our solar system. Obviously, some of the planets have many moons in orbit around them, but some of them do not have any. Mercury, Venus, the Earth, and Mars are all considered to be "terrestrial planets" which are mainly rocky and are the closest to the sun. Mercury and Venus have no moons, while the Earth has one moon and Mars has two. The four "jovian planets" which are theoretically mainly gasses; Jupiter, Saturn, Uranus, and Neptune, have many moons each. Jupiter and Saturn each have at the very least, 90 moons each (with Saturn seeming to have the most) and these numbers seem to go up on a weekly basis as we continue to discover them. Uranus has at least 28 moons, and Neptune has at least 16. We are not sure how many moons any of the gas planets actually have because we discover more and more moons as our astronomical technologies continue to increase. Those planets are a long way away. There are at least (5) five additional so-called "dwarf planets" orbiting our sun beyond Neptune that we are aware of including Pluto, which has at least three moons of its own believe it or not. There are at least (5) five moons that we know of orbiting some of the "planets" far out beyond Pluto. God is incredible!!

When it comes to the modern lie about human evolution, scientists from different backgrounds of study have fallen prey to making observational correlations and then presuming causation. A basic rule of science; "correlation is not causation", is strictly adhered to in every other genre of scientific study except for when it comes to the study of the origin of man. Big bang/evolutionary scientists blatantly ignore the fact that just because two different things are similar in some ways (people and monkeys for example), *it can never be scientifically assumed* that one of them has anything at all to do with the other one.

Most life forms on earth are comprised of billions of cells, which are themselves perfectly organized to maintain and reproduce each species (See Chapter 2; *Genetics; A Way to Understand*). God designed DNA (Deoxyribonucleic Acid) so that the descendants of each species will continue to reproduce the same DNA, thereby making more of the same species. Each species' DNA is specific to that species, yet evolutionary scientists continue to claim (without any evidence) that human beings spontaneously evolved from some other animal after that animal had evolved from something else, and so on and so forth. Modern scientists are teaching organic evolution as if it is a proven fact and it is all a filthy, demonic lie. There are of course, ***adaptational changes*** which take place ***within*** species over periods of time, but because frogs or fish which live in darker areas may have smaller eyes than those which live in more sunlit areas, this does not mean they are changing into something else. A swine is still a swine, and a hippopotamus is still a hippopotamus even though over time they may have become larger, smaller, more or less hairy, or have larger or smaller teeth, eyes, ears, etc. This is true for every species because God created life forms to be adaptable that way.

Modern scientists' explanations and interpretations of fossilized bone fragments, animal teeth, skulls, etc., are commonly presented to the public in ways which seem to support evolution as if it is a fact, but the only thing any so-called "evidence" has EVER shown is that different kinds of people; Nephilim (giant sons of Anak; Numbers

13:3 KJV), people with dwarfism, people with big heads, people with little heads, tall people, short people, etc., and pigs, bears, apes, chimpanzees, gorillas, and all sorts of other animals were all alive at some point in the past. "Transitional species" are life forms which supposedly bridge gaps between *different* species during evolutionary changes; a half-man, half-chimpanzee for example, but the fact is that there are NO transitional species anywhere and there **never** have been. There are many hoaxes and many scientific liars to perpetuate hoaxes, but there are no transitional species.

Modern scientific excuses for the lack of physical evidence to support all those evolutionary lies permeate every aspect of modern science because people can naturally understand physical facts but refuse to even try to understand spiritual truths about those same facts. The Biblical account of everything including human history is The One and Only Truth, and missing evolutionary links between human beings and monkeys or evolutionary links between other kinds of animals will always be missing ladies and gentlemen, **because they have never existed.**

Studying physical matter in detail over time can produce misleading beliefs in physicality because scientists perform physical experiments under different conditions and get the same predictable results. This makes it easy to develop a "faith" in physical consequences with zero regard to the spiritual truth about those consequences. Water is not going to spontaneously change into gasoline, lemon juice, or brake fluid because spontaneous things do not happen. God created chemical elements to be **stable**, so we can therefore make accurate experimental predictions about them even after manipulating all kinds of different variables. Atheists have come to take this stability for granted and this is what produces that "faith" in physicality. We know for instance that at room temperature, oil will not mix with water very well and that sugar will up to predictable saturation points. We can even change variables such as adding or reducing temperatures and sample amounts, and still confidently make accurate predictions about the results. That **could not happen** in a spontaneous environment. God knows what He is doing, and He knew exactly what we were going to do. God *intends* for us to investigate His incredible creations, but we need to always be aware that the "author of confusion" (the devil) is always trying to negatively influence our interpretations of those investigations.

Professional *interpretations* of scientific investigations include making new *assumptions and predictions* based on those interpretations, and this makes interpretations critical. When atheists interpret scientific study results, confusion reigns because the very author of confusion (the devil) is influencing those interpretations. Scientific assumptions and predictions based on prior study results heavily influence what is financed for further research and in modern science, most research interpretations (which again, result in new *assumptions, predictions, and theories*) are blatantly big bang/evolutionarily biased. Modern interpretations and explanations of scientific study results are therefore saturated with evolutionary dogma and scientifically unsupported foolishness. This happens in every genre of science and the devil is behind that entire mindset. This is NOT about "religion" nor "science" at all; this is about demonic denials of **THE TRUTH**.

The results of scientific investigations (when interpreted correctly) cannot be separated from The Truth of creation. Undefiled interpretations of science ALWAYS show that God created this universe and everything in it. Scientific "conclusions" which have eliminated God from the interpretations are indeed half-truths because "science" can only investigate physical matter. The **major** differences between "The Truth", "religion" (which includes Atheism, Scientology, Satanism, Buddhism, Mormonism, Christian denominations, etc.), and "scientific interpretations" are all discussed in detail in Chapter 4, "*Modern Science: Spirit Realm Research*".

Since we are supposedly the top evolutionary species in existence and the spontaneous force behind evolution is each species' survival and proliferation via natural selection, then why haven't all the animals evolved into human beings (or something even higher) after all these alleged billions of years? Why can't human beings fly? Why hasn't any land-based life form developed organic wheels? There has been more than enough time for all that to have happened based on evolutionary claims as to how long life on Earth has existed. Did spontaneous "natural selection" stop? How can similar looking, genetically different, *naturally non-interbreeding* species co-exist if they evolved from each other? How could that be? Surely mice and rats; salamanders and lizards; bluebirds and cardinals; zebras and antelope; and wildebeests and buffalo to name a few, would naturally continue to be sexual with each other. They are not because they never were! How could fossilized dinosaur footprints with human footprints **in** them exist if we did not coexist? Somebody is lying.

If you are interested in knowing The Truth, ask yourself the following questions: Since the moon is very slowly moving away from the Earth, then how can the Earth be billions of years old? How could entire schools of fish have been fossilized without there having been a major flood and then a "quick" drainage? Why are marine fossils found in mountaintops if there was no biblical flood? The giant Easter Island statues are buried up to their necks in mud and they are each about 30 feet tall. How did that happen if there was no flood? Are those statues billions of years old as well? Modern atheistic scientists claim that evolutionary changes occur in relatively short bursts of time and that transitional species do not survive for long periods of time; therefore, there are no transitional fossils. They say that as an excuse because there is not one shred of fossilized evidence of any "missing links" (even though supposedly multi-millions of species have changed over billions of years). Surely *something* transitional would have been fossilized or otherwise preserved. The *modern* atheistic excuse for this is that **all current** life forms (including humans) are transitional species currently in the process of transitioning to something else.....(try not to laugh).

Why would prey animals such as chickens, cows, worms, mice, fish, pigs, wildebeests, rabbits, etc. (which human beings and other predators have always eaten) continue to exist without having been "naturally selected" to develop defenses against consumption? *Answer*: Because God created those animals for us and other animals to eat that's why! It is utterly ridiculous to think that certain animals spontaneously naturally select themselves to be prey animals for other animals to eat. Did the fictional force of evolution also decide that human beings would not be hunted, trapped, farmed, cooked, eaten, captured for sport and placed into zoos, or held captive to be bargained over for food amongst the animals? Don't be ridiculous. It makes no sense to think that anything can be spontaneously purposed when "spontaneous" means "*without purpose*".

Early in the 1900's Anthropologists Charles Dawson and Martin A.C. Hinton intentionally filed down and changed the shapes of some fossilized animal bones they had found and then told the world the bones were from the long sought-after "missing link" in the (made-up) human evolutionary chain. They named the bones "Lucy", and the scientific community celebrated this "finding" as proof that God does not exist and that we had in fact spontaneously evolved. This made-up hoax was later shamefully revealed, and the scientific community was deservedly embarrassed. Even though this "Lucy" mess is a scientifically verified hoax, a lot of people worldwide **still believe that lie.**

The modern public is primed for this kind of hoax to be accepted at face value again because the **worldwide public** today is indeed listening to false teachers. People everywhere have itching ears they want to be continually scratched with "new" information (2 Timothy 4:3KJV) besides what The Holy Bible already tells us. There are MANY examples of lies and hoaxes throughout the scientific community regarding the fictional big bang and the theory of evolution, and instead of us wasting precious time and badly needed resources going to the moon and other celestial places to try and disprove The Holy Bible by looking for "aliens" and "signs of life", we should be going to explore this universe to glorify God by simply appreciating the many different wonders of His incredible creations!! Mankind will **never** profit by disrespecting God!

We do not know God's *original purposes* for doing **ANYTHING.** For example, why did God create Satan knowing what he was going to do? We do not know and we could not contain, nor even process that information if God WERE to tell us. We have access to all we need to know right now by The Holy Scriptures, and by The Holy Spirit for interpretation of those scriptures. Our human existences are spiritually and physically complex and we mean a lot more than any of us can understand. Human beings are eternally special, one-of-a-kind beings God created to worship Him and have dominion over this Earth and everything in it. No; we are NOT just happenstance left over star dust as the devil and his atheistic/evolutionary "modern scientists" are trying to make us believe we are! Think for yourselves and you can recognize just how incredible human beings are. May God bless you in The Name of Jesus Christ, by The Holy Spirit to understand The Truth about your existence, and may you accept God into your lives **in Jesus' Name** by The Holy Spirit. Believe in God. Trust Jesus. Rely on The Holy Spirit.

I would like to share a **powerful** thought with you which will hopefully eternally open your understanding...slow down and think about this for a moment.... Imagine we were all born and raised in Hell (all any of us have ever known is "Hell" and the things it consists of). Then when we died as believers in Jesus Christ, we came here to the Earth realm..... the differences between **EVERYTHING** here and everything in Hell would be just like God has told us the differences are between Heaven and the Earth (1 Corinthians 2:9). There is NOTHING here in this Earth-realm that a person born and raised in Hell could ever understand or relate to. They could not understand anything we would try to tell them about being in the Earth-realm because they have never heard, seen, nor could they ever imagine anything we talk about. If one of your family members were to come to you from hell crying and asking you to return to hell because they missed you, there is NO WAY that you would go back to hell. That would be an impossible decision for you to make. You could not explain ANYTHING to them such as deer, clouds, tennis shoes, bacon, music, insurance, cars, grass, worms, eggs, cartoons, windows, a drum set, mountains, biscuits, waterfalls, basketball courts, televisions, sodas … nothing. There is nothing they could relate to. They have never seen, heard, nor could have imagined anything you're talking about. You could only mention something in hell they could develop ideas about which is here (such as Jesus mentioning mansions), but that would only be a miniscule description. This is the same difference between heaven and Earth. Ever wondered why The Holy Bible mentions so little about Heaven? 1 Corinthians 2:9 in The Bible clearly explains that.

Please do not allow the devil to deceive you. God is, and salvation comes through believing in Jesus Christ and knowing He sits at the right hand of Father God and is soon to come back for His people (who worship Him in Spirit and in Truth) to take us all to Heaven; that beautiful, yet unimaginable place where we will spend eternity! HALLELUJAH!!! To GOD in the highest, in the Name of Jesus Christ by The Holy Spirit!!

Jesus Christ was a man Who is God; *Infinite and Finite at the same time.* God is before the beginning and after the end, and God did ALL of this (John Chapter 1, KJV).

God is The Reality of Everything and The Truth does indeed, speak for itself.